W9-AQG-456

RESOURCE BOOKS FOR TEACHERS

series editor
ALAN MALEY

MUSIC & SONG

Tim Murphey

43-085

Oxford University Press 1992

Oxford University Press
Walton Street, Oxford OX2 6DP

Oxford New York Toronto
Delhi Bombay Calcutta Madras Karachi
Petaling Jaya Singapore Hong Kong Tokyo
Nairobi Dar es Salaam Cape Town
Melbourne Auckland

and associated companies in
Berlin Ibadan

Oxford and *Oxford English* are a trade marks of
Oxford University Press

ISBN 0 19 437055 0

Typeset by Pentacor PLC, High Wycombe, Bucks.

Printed in Hong Kong

Acknowledgements

This book began when my two elder sisters encouraged me to sing (not always in tune!) with them as a young child, and I got hooked on music. They taught me that joy was more important than perfect pitch. For the academic background, I was helped greatly to understand the power of the medium by Jean-Paul Bronckart, Bernard Py, and Georges Denis Zimmermann, who guided my PhD research on the use of music and song in language learning.

Many other kind musical souls read and commented on previous drafts of this book, providing valuable input and encouragement. Thea Bredie, from Holland, stimulated me greatly with her initial questions and valuable comments. Rod and Sonja Nash, teaching in Germany, have corresponded with me for several years on the topic. I found Dennis Davy and his dissertation on the subject (unfortunately after I had finished my PhD on the same) and discovered a soulmate in his ideas and experience from teaching in Japan and the Arab world. Readers in Japan, teaching a variety of languages at different levels, have helped me shape the book further: Lila Madge, Felicia Rey, Gary Beaubouef, Raoul Holland, Tadashi Sakamoto, and Gabriel Yardley. Two anonymous OUP readers also gave valuable feedback. Finally, Alan Maley's engaging advice and personal interest greatly influenced the book's final form.

Several schools allowed me to experiment extensively with music and song in my classes. The Université Populaire in Neuchâtel, and the Commercial School in Biel, Switzerland were brave enough to allow me to teach 'English through music' classes. For fifteen summers at International Summer Camp, Montana, Director Rudy Studer provided me with an international mixture of children from six to eighteen years of age in our French, German, and English language courses.

During the writing I have also been fortunate to work in two extremely supportive and stimulating academic environments, at the Université de Neuchâtel in Switzerland and Nanzan University in Japan, where fellow teachers and staff have encouraged and added to the music. I would like also to thank the many individual students who taught me how to appreciate the beats of their different drums.

This book is about using music and song, and music and song were much used in its late night writing. So thanks to the music . . .

Tim Murphey
Nanzan University

The publishers and I would also like to thank the following for their permission to use copyright material:

Music & Media for the 'European Airplay Top 40'

USA Today for the article 'Voices: What do you think about the music kids are listening to today?'

Et Cetera for the article 'Pop Lyrics: A mirror and a molder of society' by Sheila Davis

Pan Books for the excerpt from *The Man who Mistook his Wife for a Hat* by Oliver Sachs.

Contents

Section 5: Video song clips

The author and series editor

Tim Murphey (BA in French and German, MA in TEFL) wrote his PhD thesis in Applied Linguistics on *Songs and music in language learning: an analysis of pop song lyrics and the use of song and music in teaching English as a foreign language* (1989). He is also the author of *Teaching One to One* (1991). He taught for seven years at the English Language Institute (University of Florida); for seven years at the Université de Neuchâtel in Switzerland; and has spent sixteen summers teaching and playing with an international array of children at International Summer Camp, Montana, Switzerland, where he co-ordinated the French, German, and English language courses. He has been teaching, writing, and learning at Nanzan University in Japan since April 1990.

Alan Maley worked for The British Council from 1962–1988, serving as English Language Officer in Yugoslavia, Ghana, Italy, France, and China, and as Regional Representative for The British Council in South India (Madras). He is currently Director-General of the Bell Educational Trust, Cambridge.

He wrote *Quartet* (with Françoise Grellet and Wim Welsing, OUP 1982). He has also written *Literature* (with Alan Duff, OUP 1990, in this series); *Beyond Words, Sounds Interesting, Sounds Intriguing, Words, Variations on a Theme,* and *Drama Techniques in Language Learning* (all with Alan Duff); *The Mind's Eye* (with Françoise Grellet and Alan Duff), and *Learning to Listen* and *Poem into Poem* (with Sandra Moulding). He is also Series Editor for the New Perspectives series, and the Oxford Supplementary Skills Series.

Foreword

There is no human society without its poetry. There is no human society without its music. When put together, they constitute a powerful force for both cultural cohesion and identity and for individual fulfilment.

In relation to language learning, the use of music and song offers two major advantages:

1 Music is highly memorable. Whether this is because it creates a state of relaxed receptivity, or because its rhythms correspond in some way with basic body rhythms, or because its messages touch deep-seated emotional or aesthetic chords, or because its repetitive patterning reinforces learning without loss of motivation— whatever the reason, songs and music 'stick' in the head.

2 It is highly motivating, especially for children, adolescents, and young adult learners. Popular music in its many forms constitutes a powerful subculture with its own mythology, its own rituals, and its own priesthood. As such it is a part of students' lives in a way that so much else we use is not. If we can tap into it, we release unsuspected positive energy.

But the appeal of music and song is not confined to the young, or to popular music alone. Folk music, opera, classical music, ethnic music—all have their devotees. The motivational appeal is present to many different types of learners.

Clearly, it would be unwise to ignore this flexible and attractive resource. Indeed, language learning has always made good use of it. This rich vein has never been quite so fully worked as in this book, however. The author sets out to prove his contention that 'anything you can do with a text you can do with a song'. But he goes beyond this to call upon the unique properties of music and song also. The result is a fascinating and varied array of material and ideas in a form highly accessible to teachers at all levels.

Alan Maley

Introduction

Once upon a time, while doing a survey in a secondary school in a remote area of Switzerland, I showed my questionnaire to the teacher before a class. One part of it had a list of the artists from the current Top 40, and she tried to identify them. Failing to recognize all but a few, she told me that her students surely would not do much better. In class, she was astonished when the students eagerly started writing song titles beside the names of nearly all the artists. As I walked around the class, I asked her to join me. On the cover of nearly every notebook and book-bag were the names and logos of the pop groups that were on the questionnaire. She had never seen them before (or had not realized what they were!). A lively discussion followed the completion of the questionnaire and the teacher was amazed at how well her students voluntarily expressed themselves in English about my research and their musical tastes and habits. From what I could see, she was a very good teacher, who had established good rapport with her students, but she had never suspected her students' intense interest in and knowledge of pop music.

A few months later, I received a letter thanking me for showing her how to tune in to her students' interests, saying she had never seen them more motivated than since she had started asking them to teach her about their music and how they perceived it. Of course, that had not been my goal at all—I was simply collecting data for my research. Her gratitude did, however, reinforce my belief that highly motivated language learning starts with the students and what they are interested in. 'As language teachers we are the most fortunate of teachers—all subjects are ours. Whatever (the students) want to communicate about, whatever they want to read about, is our subject matter.' (Rivers 1976:96)

Why this book?

Music is everywhere and all students have musical tastes. This book is intended as a tool for tapping into this resource. I also hope it will show teachers how stimulating it is to tune in to the wealth of information, reactions, and feelings already there in our students. The advantage of musical materials is that they are so readily available to the teacher, and so immediately motivational to most students.

Songs alone, however, will not teach anyone how to *use* language—no matter how great their memorability, how much fun it is to sing and listen to them, or how 'energizing' the change of pace might be. Just listening to and singing songs will not make students able to communicate in another language.

For three years I was in a choir. We learnt songs by heart in about a dozen languages that we did not speak. However, we were incapable of using the language in the songs for communication. This does not mean that we did not learn something of the sound system which might have helped us later had we studied the languages. But what we learnt in the choir could not be transferred, as it was, to natural language use.

In other words, of themselves, songs can be immensely valuable for developing certain capacities, but they can be many times more valuable if we exploit them creatively to bridge the gap between the pleasurable experience of listening/singing and the communicative use of language. That is the major goal of this book: to show how to use songs and music as enhancers, reinforcers, or as centre-pieces for communicating in the classroom. Thus, this book provides some basic starting points from which the teacher and class can diverge or progress creatively to a variety of individually adapted activities.

Finally, I hope this book will be used as a means for teachers to increase rapport with their students. Music and song is a communal activity in which, for a while, the world becomes one. Everything we see, everything we do is associated with the sound we are hearing (and which is echoing in our minds). The use of music and song in the classroom can stimulate very positive associations to the study of a language, which otherwise may only be seen as a laborious task, entailing exams, frustration, and corrections.

The importance of music and song in language learning

Many of us have experienced with amazement how quick students are at learning songs. It is also a common experience to forget nearly everything we learn in another language except the few songs that we learnt. For a variety of reasons, songs stick in our minds and become part of us, and lend themselves easily to exploitation in the classroom.

1 Although modern technology has universalized access to song, it could be that song actually preceded and aided the development of speech in *homo sapiens* (Livingstone 1973). If we think about it for a second, it is easier to put intonation on 'lalalalala' than it is to make the finer distinctions required by language, i.e. to sing with

vocalizations is significantly easier than speech. But what is even more amazing is that is also seems easier to sing language than to speak it.

2 Song also appears to precede and aid the development of language in young children (Murphey 1990a). A growing body of research indicates that the musical babbling produced by infants, and returned by parents, is extremely important in the development of language in young children.

3 I have often called songs 'adolescent motherese' (Murphey and Alber 1985). 'Motherese' is the highly affective and musical language that adults use with infants. As children grow up they get less and less of this. At adolescence, they appear to be adult and go through many changes which seem to reduce the amount of affective 'motherese' speech they receive. Songs may to a certain extent replace this, filling a need that not only adolescents have, but which all of us have throughout our lives. This affective attention, which is eventually replaced to some extent by lovers (with 'loverese'), may be lacking for many young adolescents just as their emotional systems are beginning to bloom. Their fascination with pop music may be seen as partly stemming from their need and desire for such attention. (Needless to say, somewhere in every adult there still lurks an adolescent.)

4 In our time, it is hard to escape music and song as it occupies ever more of the world around us: in operating theatres (for heart transplants and childbirth), restaurants and cafés, shopping malls (muzak), at sports events, in our cars, and literally everywhere for those tuned in to a Walkman. It would seem that the only place music and song is slow to catch on is in schools!

5 'The song stuck in my head' phenomenon (the echoing in our minds of the last song we heard after leaving our car, a restaurant, etc., and which can be both enjoyable and sometimes unnerving) also seems to reinforce the idea that songs work on our short- and long-term memory (Murphey 1990b).

6 The singing of songs resembles what Piaget (1923) described as egocentric language, in which children talk, with little concern for an addressee. They simply enjoy hearing themselves repeat. It could be that the need for egocentric language never really leaves us and is fulfilled partly through song. Krashen (1983) has suggested that this involuntary repetition may be a manifestation of Chomsky's 'language acquisition device'. It seems our brains have a natural propensity to repeat what we hear in our environment in order to make sense of it. Songs may strongly activate the repetition mechanism of the language acquisition device. It certainly seems to do so with children, who learn songs almost effortlessly.

7 Songs in general also use simple, conversational language, with a lot of repetition, which is just what many language teachers look for in sample texts. The fact that they are affective makes them many times more motivating than other texts. Although usually

simple, some songs can be quite complex syntactically, lexically, and poetically (see Sting's *Russians*, or Leonard Cohen's *Suzanne*), and can be analysed in the same way as any other literary sample.

8 Songs can be appropriated by listeners for their own purposes, largely because most pop songs (and probably many other types) do not have precise people, place, or time references. For those who find them relevant, songs happen whenever and wherever one hears them and they are, consciously or subconsciously, about the people in one's own life.

9 Most importantly, perhaps, songs are relaxing. They provide variety and fun, and encourage harmony within oneself and within a group. Little wonder they are important tools in sustaining cultures, religions, patriotism, and, yes, even revolutions.

10 In practical terms, for language teachers, songs are short, self-contained texts, recordings, and films that are easy to handle in a lesson. And the supply is inexhaustible!

The concerns of teachers

The following is a list of concerns about using music and song in the language classroom expressed by a group of commercial school teachers at the start of a two-day workshop. Items shown in italics are those most frequently stated:

1 *Administrators/teachers/students do not take music and song seriously.*
2 It disturbs neighbouring classes.
3 Some students get too excited.
4 *It takes away from the normal syllabus. Time is lost.*
5 Students disagree about songs, and have different musical tastes.
6 Pop songs have poor vocabulary—too much slang and bad grammar.
7 *How do you exploit the material usefully? What is the goal?*
8 It is hard to find lyrics—sources of 'old' recorded material are no longer available.
9 Students just want to listen, not to work.
10 Poor quality cassette/video recorder.
11 Lack of technical equipment due to cost.
12 Teachers do not like to sing or are not musical.
13 Many songs are not intelligible.
14 EFL songs are boring.
15 Students will not sing.
16 Which songs should you choose? Many express violence and sexism.
17 What to do when students bring music which teachers hate?
18 Songs go out of date very quickly.

19 How do you get other teachers involved?
20 How do you share in materials production?

The participants were asked at the end of the workshop to discuss
these concerns and to decide which were still valid. Many of these
had been dealt with during the two days and resolved. Some
concerns remain (different ones for different people), and probably
always will. No material will answer all our different needs. The
overall feeling was that the attraction of the material would
outweigh almost all criticisms of it, and that ultimately success
depended on successful manipulation of the material by the
teacher. Concern number 7 listed above (How do you exploit the
material usefully?) remained central to their reasons for attending
the workshop. It also remains central to this book.

If you are involved with a teacher's group, you may want to try this
list out with your colleagues and see which concerns they find valid,
if they would like to add anything further to the list, and what
solutions they would like to offer to any or all of them.

Music in life and music in the classroom

In my own teaching I have found it useful to remind myself of what
we do naturally with music and song (List A) and then to compare
it to what we do in the classroom with it (List B). The following
lists are not exhaustive and will be discussed in greater depth later
in the book.

List A: What do people usually do with songs or the topic of songs in everyday life?

1 Listen
2 Sing, hum, whistle, tap, and snap fingers while we listen
3 Sing without listening to any recording
4 Talk about the music
5 Talk about the lyrics
6 Talk about the singer/group
7 Talk about video clips
8 Use songs and music to set or change an atmosphere or mood, as
   'background furnishing'
9 Use songs and music to make a social environment, form a
   feeling of community, dance, make friends and lovers
10 Read about the production, performance, effect, authors,
   producers, audiences of music and song
11 Use music in dreams
12 Use music and song to make internal associations with the
   people, places, and times in our lives, so they become the
   personal soundtrack of our lives

Some people also

13 Write songs
14 Perform songs
15 Make video clips
16 Do interviews
17 Write articles
18 Do surveys, make hit lists

List B: In language teaching, anything we can do with a text we can also do with songs, or texts about songs.

In addition to 1–18 above, here are some additional things we might do with music and song in teaching.

19 Study grammar
20 Practice selective listening comprehension
21 Read songs, articles, books for linguistic purposes
22 Compose songs, articles about songs, letters to singers, questionnaires
23 Discuss a song or some aspect of 1–18 in List A
24 Translate songs
25 Write dialogues using the words of a song
26 Use video clips in many ways (see Section 5)
27 Do role-plays (as people in the song, or the artist/interviewer)
28 Dictate a song
29 Use a song for gap-fill, cloze, or for correction
30 Use music for background to other activities
31 Integrate songs into project work
32 Energize or relax classes mentally
33 Practice pronunciation, intonation, and stress
34 Break the routine
35 Do choral repetition
36 Teach vocabulary
37 Teach culture
38 Learn about your students and from your students, letting them choose and explain their music
39 Have fun.

Being natural and being schoolish

Looking at what we normally do with songs outside of classes (List A), and then looking at what we may do with them in class (List B) may provide us with many more ways of exploiting them. The B listings are not necessarily better for classroom use than those in the A group, and many in the B group may happen through just doing what comes naturally. However, we have to be careful not to kill the material by doing too much of serious B work. That is why number 39 on List B is probably the most important thing to remember when using music and song in classes.

Examples of music and song

At the manuscript stage of this book, I listed a few examples of music an/or songs for each activity. My readers did not recognize some of them and suggested others to add. That would have been fine, except that I did not know the songs they suggested! Although we were all trying to list well-known pieces, we did not know each other's selections. I realized that in order to recommend their suggested songs responsibly, I would have to find and listen to all of them. I then realized that my future readers risked not knowing my selections, and then I risked asking them to do the same thing. I did not want to give more work to teachers, but rather to facilitate their efficient and creative use of musical materials they already have. Several ideas emerged as a result:

1 Everybody has their own preferred music and songs. Our 'typical piece' in any category varies greatly.

2 We can only pick and choose what is in our environment and what is available to us.

3 Those songs coming from the students' or teachers' existing repertoire are not only easier to get hold of, but are usually more effective because we have already invested in them, emotionally, financially, and in the time spent listening to and interpreting them. I am convinced that the activities in this book can work with just about any music and songs.

4 So, the examples given after the activities reflect only one person's selection, in his environment. They are no better and no worse than those that are readily available and known to you and your students already. If you do not recognize my examples, remember, they are only examples!

This is why I have not given lists of music and songs for all styles. I assure you, the music you and your students know about already is enough, and in fact better than anybody else's list.

How to use this book

I suggest that you thumb through it first and sample an activity here and there. Refer to it when you want alternative ways of using music and song. Often the ideas outlined here will inspire you to think of variations and additions of your own. Let yourself go and do not feel you have to follow each activity to the letter. You may also discover variations that work better for certain groups or contexts in the course of trying them out. I find that each time I do an activity, I change it to fit the situation. I rarely do any activity exactly the same way twice. Also, allow your students to teach you the ways that they most enjoy exploiting their music. They come first, the activity comes second. Tune in to them first. If you do not, the best of activities will turn from harmony into cacophony.

Music and song is not really one of the conventional categories of language study (grammar, vocabulary, composition, reading, listening comprehension, conversation, etc.). But it can be the content matter of any of these categories and we can focus on any, or many, of these areas when using songs. I would recommend that you also use other books in the Resource Books for Teachers series, as well as this one, when exploiting song materials. Many of the activity types in the other books in this series apply to music and song, with a little adaptation.

How the book is organized

This book is organized around different activity types. However, I would suggest that you organize your classes around your students and the materials available (songs, music, and technical support). Having first decided on material which satisfies the interests and needs of your students and yourself, look closely at the activities section of this book and decide which methods of exploitation seem most relevant.

In some of the activities, sample texts or names of recordings are given. However, materials familiar and easily available to teachers and students will do just as well. The examples given are merely possibilities, and discerning teachers will be able to adapt, use, or change these examples to suit the specific needs and tastes of their own students.

The activities are also designed to encourage pair and small group work, in which students learn from each other as well as from the teacher and the materials, and explore their own feelings, beliefs, and perceptions. This leads to a greater degree of learner independence, involves the students more in the working of the class through their self-investment, and generally increases language acquisition.

Unless we organize our classes into normal units for conversation (small groups of two to six students), true discussion will not take place. Teachers who complain to me that students do not have ideas and that songs are not a good stimulus for discussion have usually committed the error of thinking they could stand at the front of the class and say *What do you think . . .?* Few students react, because of their natural fear of speaking up in front of a large group. After they have worked for a while in small groups, students are generally more willing to speak out because they can say *we* or even *my partner* instead of *I*—and when voicing an opinion the risk is smaller. Also because the students know that at least one other person in the room has understood them, they are more willing to risk speaking up.

Section 1 includes warm-up activities which offer you ways of 'tuning in' to the particular musical tastes of your students. The premise is that the students' choice usually makes for more effective language teaching. However, these adjustments and information-gathering activities are also authentic communication exercises in their own right.

Section 2 focuses on the use of music without words (instrumentals) and the ways in which it can be used to create an atmosphere or be central to an activity.

Section 3 looks at how student interest in the topic of music and song can be used to stimulate language learning, even if the students do not actually hear any music.

Section 4 looks at how songs can be used in the classroom as written texts and sound recordings, providing activities which go from a written text to a listening or singing activity or vice versa. The language level varies from activities suitable for beginners to advanced level students.

Section 5 examines the many ways that video clips can be exploited creatively and communicatively, emphasizing that the students remain at the centre of the activity and are never merely spectators.

Section 6 is especially written for those who teach young children (and those who are young at heart) and provides many ideas for using music and song with them. The emphasis is on materials involving action, or Total Physical Response.

The *Appendix* provides sample songs to illustrate grammatical and thematic categories, and some addresses that you might find useful.

All the activities suggested in this book have been tried and tested and work for me because my students and I have made them our own. I encourage you to make this book yours and to adapt, rewrite, cut, add to, and make the activities fit your personal style and teaching situation.

I am well aware that books usually work best for those who write them. It will work for you if you realize that what is included here is only a basic outline that is meant to be built on and developed by each one of you, together with your own classes.

Using the students and their materials

I believe that *any* songs can be useful and to some extent motivating. However, those that the students listen to already and want to hear will probably have the greatest impact on them. I would suggest two guidelines, which most of the activities in this book follow, for using songs effectively in the classroom.

1 Use the students' choice of music and songs as much as possible

Using the students' choice has several advantages:
- Music and song are 'tools for living', and the topic holds great value, especially when students select the material.
- Allowing them to choose gives them some responsibility, involves them in the lessons more, and gives school relevance to their everyday lives and concerns.
- By looking at music and song critically, with student-generated criteria, we can also help them to develop the means to sort out the good from the bad.
- For the teacher, it can be a tremendous learning experience in which the students actually teach the subject matter (their songs and music), while the teacher is a resource for the language.
- Handling material in this way equalizes the encounter between students and teachers (Thomas 1984), creating mutual respect and approximating the more equal interactions that they find outside the classroom.
- It reduces the teacher-time and work spent searching for materials which many not have as much appeal as those which students themselves contribute.

2 Keep the student at the centre of the activity

Keeping the student at the centre means that song is basically used as a catalyst to provide the student with material to manipulate in a personally relevant way. Songs are used to get inside the student, to get language out of the student. They appeal to both of Stevick's motivational axes:

The horizontal axis expresses the external aspect of his (the student's) experiences: his relations with other people, his ability to talk about past experiences, to interact with present waiters, taxi drivers and friends, and to plan for the future. This outward-looking kind of reality may in the long run be necessary for motivation, but it is not by itself sufficient. The vertical axis extends through reality that is internal to the learner: his feelings, his anxieties, and his picture of himself. (Stevick 1971)

With these axes in mind, Stevick gives the reader what he calls 'Lambert's Principle': '. . . other things being equal, a language course is effective in proportion to the breadth of its contact with the student's interests, and the depth of its penetration into his emotional life.' (ibid.) Our musical interests are usually emotionally loaded. In other words, what we are doing is insearch not input: we ask students to use their feelings, experiences, and thoughts, stimulated by the music, as the primary materials for our teaching. Exploiting these in the classroom can make our teaching more effective.

Some materials that I have seen using songs have comprehension and analysis questions. When I try to do them myself, I become somewhat annoyed because they distract rather than add to my appreciation of the song and topic. They are often trying to get the student to see the song the way the teacher does. This to me is an infringement of the student's right to free thought and interpretation. I much prefer in such instances to ask students to write comprehension and analysis questions for each other. And it is not so much in answering these questions that students learn as it is in searching for the questions they would like to ask.

For those who have never used music and song in the classroom

Whenever we try new things, we take risks. It is important to make new experiences positive and successful. This means being well prepared and only trying out things in small doses at first. Putting on some background music at the beginning or end of class or while students are doing a composition is more of an experiment than an activity. We should continually experiment with our classes to try to find the best ways for learning. Using a song cloze exercise in the last five minutes is also a relatively easy way to see if, and in what ways, music and song might increase our students' interest and motivation for learning.

After these small experiments, I would suggest following them up with the exercises for tuning in to your students' tastes (Section 1) followed by whatever suits your teaching style and your particular circumstances.

It perhaps should be noted that music and song are not being proposed here as 'the new methodology' in language classes, but rather as a tool which we can use to animate and facilitate language learning and acquisition. It is up to you and your students how much and in what ways you take advantage of what music and song have to offer.

Taking music and song seriously

In 1989–90, I did several two-day workshops on using music and song in the classroom for teachers in the Swiss professional school system. About half of the fifty particpants told me that their directors and administrators were reluctant to finance their coming, and made comments like, 'What does music and song have to do with language learning?'

The teachers also complained of getting the same reactions from fellow teachers, and even the students themselves on occasions.

Music and song can be as useful as, and sometimes more than, conventional classroom materials. But it is often suspect because it is so enjoyable and so little used. Louis-Jean Calvet (1980) says that the idea that language learning cannot be enjoyable is outdated. Nevertheless, many teachers and students cling to the attitude that if something is fun, you cannot be learning. Like medicine, these people think, if it does not taste nasty, it cannot be doing you any good.

This book attempts to show otherwise.

1 Tuning in

This section demonstrates how teachers can tune in to their students' interests and become sensitive to their tastes. Feedback from students can then be developed and used in later classes. Although it is always reassuring to know in advance about our students' interests so that we can find and prepare suitable materials, the process of getting to know them and their tastes can become an integral and communicative part of the course.

There is a wealth of song material that has worked with young children for a number of years. With adolescents and adults, however, material used successfully one year may become dry and irrelevant the next. Whereas young children usually accept any kind of music and song, especially when they are allowed and encouraged to move with it, adolescents are already using their own music as a vehicle for group identity and self-discovery. They often reject dated music (even if it is only a year old), as being what their parents and older siblings listen to. On the other hand, they may nostalgically embrace rock n' roll, sixties music, or jazz. Tuning in to their tastes, new or old, can be both enjoyable and useful, as it promotes natural interaction in the classroom. Using students' own selections, which they can bring to you on cassette, together with lyrics sheets, reduces your preparation time and provides you with a large stock of material. (See activity 1.10 on how to generate materials.)

Activities in this section (unless otherwise stated) should be workable with young adolescents (11 and 12 year-olds) as well as adults, with slight modifications at either end of the spectrum.

As in other sections, one of the main purposes of the activities is to allow teachers to learn from their students and to understand how they perceive and use music.

1.1 Musical introduction cards

LEVEL	**All levels**
TIME	**5–10 minutes** (at the beginning of class)
AIM	To familiarize new students with each others' names and their musical preferences; to encourage questions and answers about likes.

PREPARATION   1 Bring to class some index cards (postcard size, one for each student in the class) and some straight pins to pin the cards to the students' shirts.

2 Find a recording of some lively music. Set up your cassette player in the classroom and make sure it is working.

IN CLASS   1 Ask students to fill in their card. Show them an example on the overhead projector (OHP), or on the board. For example:
- first name in the middle
- a favourite style of music in the upper right-hand corner
- a favourite song in the upper left-hand corner
- a favourite group or singer in the bottom left-hand corner
- an old song, group, or singer that they like in the bottom right-hand corner.

SAMPLE CARD

```
  Let it Be              Rock n' Roll


              Mari


  Paula Abdul            Dire Straits
```

2 Turn on some lively music (any music that will create a party atmosphere and encourage students to move) and let the students walk around, introduce themselves, and read each other's card.

3 When the music stops, they ask the person they are with a question about the information on their card.

4 Start the music again as soon as you see that most pairs have had enough time to ask a question and get an answer.

VARIATION 1   Collect the cards from the students. Give them out at random to different students, who have to write a paragraph about the person on the card. If they do not understand the information, they find the person who wrote the card and interview them about it. (The writing part of this activity could be done for homework.)

VARIATION 2	On the back of cards students write questions about the information on the front, for example, *Who wrote 'Oh Suzanna'?* The cards are then returned to the original writer for answering.
VARIATION 3	After the first day, name tags can be displayed on a poster or wall and students invited to read them during breaks.
VARIATION 4	A game can be played in which one student goes to the collection of name cards, chooses one piece of information and says something like *I know someone who likes the song 'Oh Suzanna'*. The rest of the class has to guess the person's name. (This variation can be done individually or in teams.)

1.2   Pop picture collage

LEVEL	**All levels**
TIME	**15–20 minutes**
AIM	To practise describing people.
PREPARATION	For homework, ask your students to bring to class one or two cuttings from magazines about singers or groups.
IN CLASS	1 Ask the students to display the cuttings on the wall. Tell them that each picture should touch another; this makes for a more interesting collage. You can then select one or several of the variations below.
	2 Ask students to work in pairs and to take turns to describe different pictures to their partners, without saying the name of the artist (if they know it). When the partner guesses correctly (*It's the man underneath Madonna, on the left*) they change over.
VARIATION 1	Ask students to write a short descriptive paragraph about one of the people in the pictures (preferably one they do not know), making it a purely physical description, and never naming the person. They should not give away the identity too soon, so that it takes the readers (other classmates) time to guess who it is. When they have all finished, the students walk around and read each others' descriptions and guess who the people are.
VARIATION 2	Students give short presentations on the picture they brought in, and confirm or disagree with the descriptions given by other students. Encourage questions from the class.

VARIATION 3	To practise reported speech, ask the students to work in pairs and to give a short presentation to each other on the subject of the picture they brought in. The students report back to the class or to a new partner what their first partner said about the picture.
VARIATION 4	The level of the activity can be raised by asking the students to make further suppositions about the lifestyle and feelings of the person in the picture, for example: *She looks as if she had just . . . She probably lives . . . She probably likes to eat . . . Her favourite food is probably . . .* At the end of this activity, you can display the descriptions around the collage for the students to read from time to time.

1.3   Pop picture twenty questions

LEVEL	**All levels**
TIME	**5–15 minutes**
AIM	To practise giving descriptions.
PREPARATION	Ask your students to bring to class one or two more cuttings from magazines about singers and groups. Alternatively, you could collect as many postcards of pop stars as there are students in your class. It is worth pasting magazine cuttings onto cards so that they will last. This will then become your pop picture resource library.
IN CLASS	**1** A nice lead in to this activity, in case any of your students are not familiar with the activity, is for you to demonstrate it at the front of the class, with a student holding up a picture so that the rest of the class can see it (but you cannot), and you asking questions. With low-level classes, you may wish to prime the students with some question cues:

Yes/no **questions**
– *Is it a woman?*
– *. . . colour picture?*
– *. . . outside?*
– *Is he/she . . . old/singing/standing/looking at the camera/happy/ wearing nice clothes/alone?*
– *Does he/she have blond hair/blue eyes/a guitar/long hair/a lot of hits?*
– *Is it Madonna/an American?* etc.

Wh- **questions**
– *Where does he/she come from?*
– *What exactly is he/she wearing?*
– *Where is the picture taken?*
– *What is in the background?*
– *What is the expression on the singer's face?* etc.

2 Let each student choose a card and pair off with another student, making sure that their partner does not see the picture. First one and then the other asks ten *yes/no* questions about the artists. The student answering must remember to say *yes* or *no* only, and not comment further.

3 When each pair has asked the ten *yes/no* questions, they can make one guess. Then they ask ten *wh*-questions (*Where is he/she famous? When was he/she born? What kind of music does he/she play?*) and guess again at the end.

VARIATION 1

1 As they question each other, ask the students to take notes of the answers. After they have had their turn asking the questions, they must write a description, or draw a picture of what is on the card (without ever having seen it), even if they know who it is.

2 After they have written their description, their partner reads it and decides if it is accurate, correcting any misunderstandings by showing the card.

VARIATION 2

The descriptions from Variation 1 can be put randomly up on the wall with the written cards lower down, the first numbered 1, and the pictures lettered from A. Students read the descriptions and try to match them with the cards.

1.4   Hit chart

LEVEL

False beginners to advanced

TIME

20–30 minutes

PREPARATION

Ask your students to find you a local, regional, or international hit chart. Prepare a questionnaire with comprehension and other questions based on it (see Sample Questionnaire below).

IN CLASS

1 Circulate the chart and ask the students to notice exactly what it is:
– *Is it an Airplay chart* (from radio airplay) *or a sales chart?*
– *Is it for singles, albums, or compact discs* (CDs)?
– *Is it a pop, rock, black, country, or other chart?*

2 Ask questions that will help your students with the questionnaire you have prepared for them. In the sample chart below they need to focus on things such as the date of the chart, what the circled numbers mean, and why each song has three numbers beside it.

3 Hand out the questionnaire and ask the students to answer it individually or in pairs.

4 When they have finished (or after ten minutes or so), let students compare answers and discuss.

HIT CHART

MUSIC & MEDIA

European *Airplay Top 40*

April 29, 1989

THIS WEEK	LAST WEEK	WKS ON CHARTS	TITLE Artist- Original Label (Publisher)	THIS WEEK	LAST WEEK	WKS ON CHARTS	TITLE Artist- Original Label (Publisher)
1	1	6	**Like A Prayer** Madonna-Sire (Various)	(21)	39	2	**You On My Mind** Swing Out Sister - Fontana (10/Oblique/Copyright Ctl)
(2)	6	16	**She Drives Me Crazy** Fine Young Cannibals-London (Virgin Music)	22	17	7	**End Of The Line** The Traveling Wilburys - Wilbury Record Co. (Copyright Control)
(3)	5	13	**The Way To Your Heart** Soulsister-EMI (EMI Music Publ.)	(23)	34	3	**Beauty's Only Skin Deep** Aswad-Mango (Jobete Music)
4	3	8	**Eternal Flame** The Bangles-CBS (Various)	24	20	5	**Sans Logique** Mylene Farmer-Polydor (B. Le Page/Polygram)
(5)	8	4	**The Look** Roxette-Parlophone (Jimmy Fun Music)	25	15	7	**Help** Bananarama/Lananeeneenoonoo-London (Northern Songs)
6	7	6	**Straight Up** Paula Adbul-Virgin (Virgin Music/Wolff Music)	26	14	11	**Kokomo** The Beach Boys-Elektra (Campbell/Connelly)
7	2	14	**You Got It** Roy Orbison-Virgin (SBK/Orbisongs Music)	(27)	43	2	**This Is Your Land** Simple Minds - Virgin (Virgin Music)
(8)	12	7	**This Time I Know It's For Real** Donna Summer-Warner Brothers (All Boys Music/ EMI Music)	28	2	4	**She's A Mystery To Me** Roy Orbison - Virgin (U2/Warner Chappell)
9	11	6	**Too Many Broken Hearts** Jason Donovan-PWL (All Boys Music)	29	26	4	**People Hold On** Coldcut-Ahead Of Our Time (Big Life/Block & Gilbert)
10	4	5	**Ordinary Lives** Bee Gees-Warner Brothers (Gibb Brothers/BMG/PRS)	(30)	38	2	**Looking For Freedom** David Hasselhoff-White Records/BMG Ariola (Young Musikverlag)
11	13	8	**Celebrate The World** Womack & Womack-4th & B'way (Copyright Control)	(31)	40	2	**If You Don't Know Me By Now** Simply Red - WEA (Mighty Three/Island)
12	9	14	**Something's Gotten Hold of My Heart** Marc Almond-EMI (Dick James Music)	32	31	4	**Baby I Don't Care** Transvision Vamp-MCA (Cinepop Music)
(13)	21	3	**When Love Comes To Town** U2-Island (Blue Mountain-Chappell)	33	32	15	**Love Train** Holly Johnson-MCA (Warner Bros)
(14)	29	3	**Good Thing** Fine Young Cannibals - London (Cambell/Connelly)	34	27	8	**International Rescue** Fuzzbox - WEA (Warner Chappell/Southern)
15	16	3	**The Beat(en) Generation** The The-Epic (The The Music/10 Music)	35	37	7	**Y'A Des Bons** Jeanne Mas-EMI (MAS Music)
16	10	9	**Leave Me Alone** Michael Jackson-Epic (Warner Chappell Music)	(36)	50	19	**Stop** Sam Brown-ASM (Ronder/Wayblue/C. Contr.)
(17)	28	15	**The Living Years** Mike & The Mechanics- WEA (Rutherford/R&BA/Hit&Run)	37	36	4	**Don't Be Cruel** Bobby Brown-MCA (Cal-Gene/Virgin/MCA)
(18)	30	4	**I Beg Your Pardon** Kon Kan - Atlantic (Bun/Warner Chappell)	38	18	6	**I'd Rather Jack** Reynolds Girls-PWL (All Boys Music)
(19)	35	3	**Americanos** Holly Johnson-MCA (Warner Chappell/4Loves.)	39	41	2	**Sarbacane** Francis Cabrel-CBS (Ed. Musicale Chandelle)
20	23	11	**I Don't Want A Lover** Texas-Mercury (10 Music)	40	19	24	**Twist In My Sobriety** Tanita Tikaram-WEA (Brogue/Warner Chappell)

**SAMPLE
QUESTIONNAIRE**

Work in pairs. Look at the hit chart and
first discuss the following questions:

- *What do you think the circles mean?*
- *What does 'Airplay' mean?*
- *What do the three numbers next to each
  song title mean?*

Now answer the questions below:

1 How many songs in the chart are climbing?
2 Which song has been in the chart the
   longest?
3 Which song was number 13 last week?
4 Which song has been in the chart for three
   weeks and has risen 15 places since last
   week?
5 If the song *Stop* climbs as much next week
   as it did last week, at what position will it be
   in the 6 May chart?

6 Which song rose the most this week?
7 How many songs in the chart are in French?
8 Which singer in the chart died in 1990? (Clue:
   he had a top 10 hit and is in the chart twice.)
9 Which of the songs have you heard before?
10 Which of the songs do you have at home?
11 Which songs have you heard or seen on
   video clips?
12 On a scale of 1–10 (1 = no, 10 = yes), to what
   extent do you agree with the words in the
   titles of numbers 9 and 23?
13 Which songs from the chart do you like best?
14 Which song that you *do not* know would you
   now like to listen to (out of curiosity)?
15 Which of your favourite songs *not* in the chart
   do you think should be? Give the titles and
   the names of the artists.

VARIATION 1   Look through the first few questions with the whole class until the
students understand what they have to do.

VARIATION 2   The students themselves can make up a different set of questions.

REMARKS   This activity can be used to practise the full range of verb tenses (as
in the example) or specific ones that you want to stress. The type of
questions can also be adapted to the level of the class. (See also
activities 3.10 and 3.11.)

1.5 Music questionnaires

LEVEL   **All levels**

TIME   **15–45 minutes**

AIM   To provide oral and written practice in answering questions.

PREPARATION   Prepare simple questions about listening habits, uses of music, and
preferences. You can either prepare a hand-out or ask the questions
orally. Questions can be easy *yes/no* types or open-ended for the
more advanced. Parts or all of the sample questionnaires at the end
of this activity could be used.

IN CLASS

1 Go over the questions first to make sure they are all understood. Tell the students not to put their names on the questionnaires.

2 Ask the students to work in pairs to fill out the questionnaires with information about each other. In doing this, each has to ask the other the questions, and thus a good deal of interaction is encouraged.

3 Collect the questionnaires and ask a few (volunteer) students to tabulate the results for homework and to report back to the class.

VARIATION 1

False beginners
Ask the males and the females in the class to do their questionnaires separately, tabulate the results according to gender, then compare the two.

VARIATION 2

Devise shorter questionnaires to obtain specific information with particular groups, or to be used as ice-breakers or one-minute break ideas.

VARIATION 3

1 Cut up a questionnaire (see Sample Questionnaire 2) and give one question to each student in the class.

2 Each student asks all the other students in the class the question (or asks just the males, or just the females) and tabulates the results.

3 The students then write a summary and report orally back to the class. In a very large class, give one question per pair. One student asks the questions, the other acts as secretary or 'scribe'. Then they both write a short report along the lines: *Our question was . . . . We found that 80 per cent of the women we asked . . . .*

4 The results of the oral presentations can be recorded on the board. The male/female survey results can also be compared.

5 After discussion, the students can individually or in groups write a paragraph on what they think are the most interesting findings.

VARIATION 1

Intermediate and advanced
When the students have finished their questionnaires take them in. Shuffle them and hand them back randomly. Students read and try to guess who filled them in. They circulate and ask questions to find out whose paper it is. They continue to ask the same person questions until they get a negative response. (Some people will, of course, have the same answers.)

VARIATION 2

Students may want to make up their own questionnaire, asking the questions they are especially interested in.

VARIATION 3

Students try to guess what the results might be with another group (older or younger). If such a group is available, students may want to carry out a survey to see if their predictions were correct.

VARIATION 4

Students fill in the questionnaire for their partner without asking them any questions, to see how well they know each other. They speculate about the musical habits of their partner and then compare and discuss. (Speculations can be in pencil, real answers in ink.)

VARIATION 5

A questionnaire can be taken out to larger groups for comparison (teachers in the school, other classes, employers, etc.)

VARIATION 6

Out of class, the students can question someone who speaks the target language. They may want to record the interview and play it back for the class.

VARIATION 7

The questionnaire can be used as the basis for a newsletter. Different students are assigned the task of writing about the answers to different questions on the questionnaire and trying to interpret the results (see also 1.7).

REMARKS

Any question or group of questions (A, B, C, or D) from the following questionnaire could be used for the above activities. The questionnaire should only be used in its entirety with an advanced class. Again, it may be more fun to let students make up their own questions.

SAMPLE
QUESTIONNAIRE 1

Part A
1 Age? ...
2 M/F? ...
3 Mother tongue? ...
Other languages spoken? ...
Example:
Do you play an instrument?
4 play/instrument? Which one(s)? ...
5 sing/choir? ...
6 read/music? ...
7 sing/shower? ...
8 wake up/music? ...
9 go to sleep/music? ...
10 study/listen/music? ...
11 play/played/band? ...
12 take/dance lessons? What kind? ...
13 do/aerobics? ...
14 write/song(s)? ...
15 read/pop music magazines? Which ones? ...

Part B
Give answers in minutes and/or hours per day.
Example:
How many minutes/hours a day do you listen to the radio?
16 listen/radio? ...
17 listen/cassettes/CDs/LPs? ...

18 watch/music videos on TV? ...
19 watch/other programmes on TV? ...
20 What percentage (approximately) of the songs that you listen to are:
• instrumentals? ... %   • in English? ... %
• in other languages? ... %

Part C
Circle the answer which is true for you.
21 Do you play the same song several times?
•never   •sometimes   •often   •very often
22 Do you choose music to suit your activity?
•never   •sometimes   •often   •very often
23 Do you use music just for background?
•never   •sometimes   •often   •very often
24 Do you listen to classical music?
•never   •sometimes   •often   •very often
25 Does music ever disturb you?
•never   •sometimes   •often   •very often
If yes, when and why? ...

Part D
Example:
How often do you buy an LP record?
(once a week/fortnight/month/year/never)
26 buy/LP record? ...
27 buy/CD? ...
28 buy/single? ...

**SAMPLE
QUESTIONNAIRE 2**

1	Do you play an instrument? Which one(s)? ...	**12**	Do you read pop music magazines? Which ones?...
2	Do you sing in a choir? Have you ever sung in a choir?	**13**	Do you like to sing karaoke?
3	Can you read music?	**14**	How often do you use a Walkman? (never/sometimes/often/very often)
4	Do you sing in the shower or bath?	**15**	Do you listen to music:
5	Do you wake up to music?		a. less than an hour a day
6	Do you go to sleep with music?		b. more than an hour a day
7	Do you study with music?		c. more than two hours a day?
8	Do you play in a band? Have you ever played in a band?	**16**	Do your parents like the music you listen to?
9	Do you take dance lessons? What kind? ...	**17**	Of the songs that you listen to are:
10	Do you go to discos? (never/sometimes/often/very often)		a. less than 25%
			b. more than 25%
11	Have you ever written a song/songs?		c. more than 50%
			d. more than 75% in English?

1.6   Music survey

LEVEL

Intermediate to advanced

TIME

30–60 minutes ($\times 3$)
This activity requires 30–60 minutes' class time to decide what
questions to ask and how to tabulate the results; 30–60 minutes'
out-of-class time to ask the questions and record the results; and a
follow-up period of 30–60 minutes to report results and write up a
summary.

AIM

To develop student questioning skills and report writing. To gather
information for later use.

PREPARATION

Make photocopies of previous class reports or reports of statistics in
music magazines. Prepare the students by giving them a list of
possible topics/questions to ask. You may choose to use or adapt the
Sample Questionnaires in 1.5. Below is an example of the kind of
survey form your students may write.

IN CLASS

1 The students decide which questions to ask, in groups of two or
three. Check their questions.

2 The students work out what kind of answers they want (*yes/no*/on
a scale/open ended, etc.), and prepare question sheets for the
answers.

3 If the students decide to tape-record the answers (beginners can ask simple questions, such as *What do you think of Madonna?*), they can bring back their recordings and listen to them in class.

4 The students then agree on how many subjects to interview and what category of subjects they will approach (only girls between 16 and 18, or only teachers, for example).

VARIATION 1

The survey can be done within the class, with another class, with a selected group of people in the school, or in the community (for example, with parents, friends, neighbours, etc.).

VARIATION 2

The students can write up the results as articles for publication in a newsletter (see activity 1.7).

SAMPLE SURVEY FORM

> # Music survey
> 1   Do you like heavy metal? (yes/no/not sure)
> 2   What do you think of his/her music?
>   1 = terrible, 7 = excellent
>   Madonna   1 2 3 4 5 6 7
>   Sting   1 2 3 4 5 6 7 etc.
> 3   Who is your favourite group or artist?
> 4   What do you think of Michael Jackson?

REMARKS

1 Students may want to 'borrow' questions from the music questionnaires, but in general it is best for them to think up their own questions.

2 This activity is a good follow-up to the music questionnaires in 1.5.

1.7   Music newsletter

LEVEL

Intermediate to advanced

TIME

30–60 minutes (×2)

AIM

To practise journalistic writing from bare facts. To reinforce and follow up previous group work with a publication.

PREPARATION

Prepare and copy the sample hand-out below.

IN CLASS

Lesson 1

1 Give each student a copy of the hand-out you have prepared.

2 Hold a brainstorming session for students to decide what they wish to write about and how. (They may want a co-author or they may prefer to work alone.) Hold this session a few days before the actual composing to allow the students time to think about it and to ask other people for ideas.

3 Two or three editors can be chosen to do the layout.

Lesson 2

1 When composing starts, encourage the students to get feedback first from each other and then from you.

2 Depending on the group, they can decide whether to keep the articles in their own writing, or type them up, or put them on a word processor before actually copying the newsletter. Several students may wish to act as editors and do the layout as well, or you may wish to organize this as a class activity.

SAMPLE HAND-OUT

• • • • • *Calling all music lovers!* • • • • •

Today is Monday. At the end of this week you are going to write an article for a music newsletter. You should decide on the topic for your article today, then think about it and gather information during the week. We will print 100 copies of the newsletter next week. You can compose it in or out of class. You can have a co-author or do it alone. It can be humorous or serious. A few possible topics are listed here:

• Top 10 (survey report)
• Do you like ...? (survey report)
• What do you think of ...? (survey report)
• An interview with someone about music
• An imaginary interview with a star
• An editorial about some aspect of the music scene (music, video clips, fashion, drugs, image, etc.)
• A summary of an article taken from another magazine
• A commentary on an artist or song that you particularly like.

VARIATION 1

The students may want to institutionalize the newsletter and appoint student editors to publish it once a term.

VARIATION 2

The newsletter can be in several different languages and involve teachers from the different language courses. This stimulates a natural desire for translation. Students may want to help you to understand articles in other languages!

REMARKS

Activities 1.5 and 1.6 and reading articles from music magazines in English are good lead-ins. Students may want to invent an interview, report an actual concert or recent hit parade, or write an editorial on some aspect of the music scene. These will be better understood if examples are available for them to consult.

**SAMPLE
NEWSLETTER**

SPEAKING OF MUSIC

INTERNATIONAL SUMMER CAMP MONTANA SWITZERLAND 15 JULY
A report by the English Class Research Team after a survey of 40 Senior girls and 15 boys.

• Campers' Top 10

Senior boys and girls have very different musical tastes. Girls listen to twice as many different groups as the boys. Also, a singer's popularity changes a lot from the boys to the girls.

Madonna, even with all her problems with Sean Penn and Nick Kamon is only no. 4 with the girls and no. 1 with the boys.

Genesis, however, won by 4 points the first place in the girls' top 10 but is second with the boys.

Dire Straits and their cross between new age and rock is more popular with girls than with boys.

• Boys' Top 10

1 Madonna
2 Genesis
3 Bruce Springsteen
4 Simple Minds
5 The House Martins
6 Bon Jovi
7 Modern Talking
8 Duran Duran
9 Michael Jackson
10 Sting

• Girls' Top 10

1 Genesis
2 Depeche Mode
3 U2
4 Communards
5 Erasure
6 Dire Straits
7 Duran Duran
8 Madonna
9 The Police
10 Bruce Springsteen

• Disturbing Music?

Several questions asked if we played songs repeatedly and chose music for different activities. As expected almost everyone does this sometimes. Asked whether music ever disturbed them, all of the campers replied 'Never!'. Another interesting find was that 30% of the girls never listen to classical music and nearly 50% of the boys never listen to Jazz. But then, neither do I.

• Musical Habits

by Irene
Hello!!
I'm going to tell you about your musical habits. I think it is very interesting, so read on!! Fewer Senior boys sing in a choir than girls, as little as 10%. However most of the people that come to camp are musical. Incredibly, we found that 50% of the girls read music and 35% of the boys! Even more fantastic, most of us wake up to music (75% of the girls, and 50% of the boys).

In our questionnaire we can see that people like to study with music very much. Lastly, almost everyone likes to sing in the shower. Do you know why? Think about it.

1.8 Star reports

LEVEL   **Intermediate to advanced**

TIME   **One or more classes**

AIM   To practise report-writing skills.

PREPARATION   Prepare some guidelines for the students (as in the Sample Hand-out) on how to go about writing their reports—the questions they should address, length of presentation, visuals, whether to include a song by the artist, and how to prepare hand-outs for the rest of the class.

IN CLASS   1 Tell the students that their reports should be kept short (5–15 minutes) and the presentation should be varied (it could include playing music, talking about the star, or acting out a mock interview).

2 Hand out the guidelines in the first lesson and ask the students to sign up, each for a different artist or group.

3 The presentations can be given every day or one a week, at the end of the class.

VARIATION   You may wish to have a written report beforehand, but should encourage free speaking instead of reading. Visuals can be displayed in the classroom after the presentation.

REMARKS   This activity may be more stimulating if done in pairs, but you should stress that each of the partners must particpate (speak) for approximately the same amount of time. The students may want to take turns as in a TV news programme.

SAMPLE HAND-OUT

Star reports

1 Presentation time: 5-15 minutes
2 Reports should include: a short biography; record history; visual; remarks on music and lyrics; pictures; a short song or musical excerpt of not more than three minutes, and lyrics (to be distributed to the class).

3 You should also prepare a short exercise for the class to do, for example, a gap-fill, comprehension questions, opinions on topics, a crossword, etc.
4 Sign up for the date of your presentation this week.
5 See your teacher after class for a few minutes, *a week before* your presentation, to show what you have prepared.

1.9   Extreme opinions

LEVEL	Intermediate to advanced
TIME	20–40 minutes
AIM	To get students to question what they and others think, and to discuss these different perspectives in the target language.
PREPARATION	Prepare a list of *extreme opinions* on music and song. Make them so extreme that you yourself would have trouble agreeing with any of them out of context. (See the examples below aimed at intermediate and intermediate to advanced pupils respectively.)

EXAMPLE 1

A What kind of person would make each of the statements below?
B Are they ever true?
C Change each sentence so that you can agree with it.
1 The Walkman is dangerous.
2 Classical music is the best music.
3 You cannot study if you are listening to music.
4 Old people do not like modern music.
5 Musicians are alcoholics and drug addicts.
6 Everybody can sing.
7 Music magazines tell the truth about stars.
8 Video clips are like junk food.

EXAMPLE 2

A What kind of person would make each of the statements below?
B Is there any truth at all in each statement? (a little/lot?)
C Change each sentence so that you could agree with it.
1 Music is the international language of humanity.
2 Rock n' roll music leads to alcohol and drugs.
3 Old people cannot appreciate new music.
4 Classical music is the purest form of music.
5 Either people are musical or not. They are born with it, it is a gift, and no amount of study or work will change that.
6 Children should be forced to sing and memorize songs in school.
7 The Walkman is an isolating and anti-social invention.
8 At its least harmful, music is simply distracting noise pollution. At its worst, it is a politically chauvinistic and commercially manipulative stimulant.
9 Music provokes wild, uncontrolled dancing and anti-social behaviour.
10 Music is a drug and should be limited by law.

IN CLASS

1 First go over each statement briefly for comprehension and problem vocabulary.

2 The students form pairs and ask each other the following questions:
- *What kind of person would say such a thing?*
- *Is there any truth in the statement?*
- *How would you modify it for yourself, or do you think it is acceptable as it is?*

The pairs should try to reach some sort of agreement between them.

3 Finally, go through the list of opinions, asking volunteers to report to the rest of the class what each pair thought about the statements. However, anyone who would like to should be allowed to comment when they feel like it. It is important to stress at the beginning of the activity that no opinion is wrong, but that the students should be able to support what they say with some sort of argument.

VARIATION 1

Point 2 above could be done in writing.

VARIATION 2

After the pairs have gone through the list, they could form new pairs and report what they decided with their first partner.

VARIATION 3

The statements could be taken out of the classroom as interview-stimulus questions. Anyone could be interviewed, but the most interesting would be musicians themselves (pop, classical, jazz, or other), school music teachers, and music critics. The students could then do a follow-up report in class on the points of view they had elicited.

VARIATION 4

The list could also be used for an arguing game in which one half of each group of four are optimists and the other half are pessimists. They have to volley back and forth, countering each others' arguments.

REMARKS

If this activity is sensitively carried out, it can help you to understand your students' individual points of view, help them to express themselves openly, and encourage rapport between you!

1.10 Weekly song rota

LEVEL

All levels

TIME

Part of two classes

AIM

To collect motivating and pedagogically useful material selected by students themselves.

PREPARATION 1   1 Prepare a hand-out similar to the one in the example below.

          2 Make enough copies for all your students.

IN CLASS   1 Give each student a hand-out.

2 Ask students to sign up on your volunteer form agreeing to bring in a song of their choice, on cassette, together with a copy of the lyrics (or the words written out to the best of their ability). They should also provide some short comments about the singer/group's history, image, etc., and perhaps say why they chose the song. (See example of volunteer sheet below.)

**SAMPLE
HAND-OUT**

Using your songs in class

In response to the question *How would you like to study English?* most of you said that you would like to use songs part of the time. I agree, but I think the best songs to use are yours, so I would like to ask your help in collecting materials. The idea is as follows:

Every week, for the next ten weeks, two of you will give me one of your favourite songs on video or audio cassette, with some or all of the following:

1 A copy of the lyrics if available. If not, the lyrics written out to the best of your ability.

2 Magazine pictures and LP covers, cuttings, and articles about the singer or group.

3 A short background history of the artist(s) (as much as you know).

4 Reasons for choosing the song and the artist – what you like about them, and why other people might like the song, or why you think they should know about it.

5 What language it presents: idioms, vocabulary, slang, grammar, and whether it is easy or difficult, etc.

6 How you think the song could be used in class:
   - for enjoyment
   - for idioms
   - to make us speak about an important social topic.
   - for vocabulary
   - for pronunciation

Materials should be handed in to me on Wednesdays so that I have time to look at them and prepare them for use the following week. I will return them to you when we have finished. Do you agree?

SAMPLE FORM

Volunteer form for song materials

Class ... .
To reserve a song spot please write in the title (and artist) under your name as soon as you have decided.

Name ....

Artist(s)...

Song ....

18 April..

25 April..

2 May ....

PREPARATION 2	When the students give you their songs, prepare them for use with any of the activities in this book, or copy the lyrics and student notes and let the students read/sing along and enjoy the activity itself. I found students really like reading each others' comments, and seeing their work distributed to others. Many of the activities in this book could be used with the songs, but for some quick possibilities, see below.
VARIATION 1	Before copying the lyrics, blank out the first few letters in the left-hand margin or down the middle of the text. It is not uncommon for me to receive a faulty photocopy of an article in which the first few letters are missing and I then have to read and fill them in from the context. Students find it useful and enjoyable to read the whole sentence and work out from the context what the missing words/ letters are.
VARIATION 2	Blank out selected words.
VARIATION 3	Dictate the first verse of the song.
VARIATION 4	Ask students to listen first and write down as many words as they can. Then give them the lyric sheets for them to check.
REMARKS	In my university classes, I did this with two of the five groups that I taught in 1990. I found that I could often use the songs in different ways with the other groups as well, thus saving precious preparation time. My students took me up on the 'some or all of the following' and provided cassette, lyrics, and a page of written notes.

1.11   Favourite song roll call

LEVEL	**All levels**
TIME	**10 minutes** (or more depending on the use of variations)
AIM	To practise listening and dictation skills.
PREPARATION	None.
IN CLASS	1 When you call each person's name, ask them to respond with the title of one of their favourite songs. Each person should respond with a different song, so the students need to have several songs in mind in case the person before them says the title they have chosen. 2 The others in the class write down the titles as each person says it. Thus, everyone is giving a dictation to everyone else. This in itself is an interesting thing to do, and will spark a lot of talk. You can leave it at that or try one of the variations below.

VARIATION 1   Class lists with the students' names can be distributed to all the students and they can write the titles beside the names as they say it. After finishing they can get up and ask each person
a.   For confirmation of the words and spelling,
b.   Who the artist is,
c.   Why they chose the song. They may also ask any combination of the three or other questions that you or they might think of.

VARIATION 2   Ask the students to write a story or dialogue with the song titles (see 3.10).

VARIATION 3   You can ask them to do a grammatical analysis of the titles (see 3.16).

2 Just music

Music has the potential to change the atmosphere in a classroom. It seems to give energy where there was none, and to spark off images when students complain of having nothing to write about. 'Music is the stuff dreams grow on.' (Tanak Akay 1900). Mood music is very popular now, whether in the dentist's surgery to relax us, or in shopping centres to encourage us to buy. Heart surgeons now use music to relax operating teams during long and stressful operations. In one London hospital women can listen to music on a Walkman during childbirth to relax them. It is only a matter of time before teachers catch on to the powerful effect that music can have on a student's performance, whether it is used as background or foreground to composition, reading, and discussion, in language classes or in other subject areas. One teaching method (Suggestopaedia) already uses background music as an integral part of the course.

A note about Suggestopaedia

Suggestopaedia, a teaching methodology developed by Dr Lozanov in Bulgaria, claims to produce hypermnesia—an excellent memory. Among its many innovations is the use of background music during the reading of dialogues (of which the students have the text and a translation). The dialogue is usually read twice, once slowly and once at normal speed, to the accompaniment of background classical music and at about the same volume. The idea behind using the music is apparently to relax students' defences and to open up their minds to the language. Music may also engage the right hemisphere of their brains more, and make learning a more holistic experience. (For further information on Suggestopaedia, see the background reading list in the Bibliography.)

Although you do not have to be a Suggestopaedia teacher to use background music, Suggestopaedia does provide a precedent for its use in the language class. Some of the activities that follow can be done with either instrumental music or songs with lyrics. Experiment with your students to see how they react to just music or songs.

2.1   Starting with music

LEVEL

All levels

TIME

5–10 minutes (at the beginning of a class)

AIM

To set a certain mood, to relax or excite students (depending on the music), or to liven up a classroom that may be depressingly silent.

PREPARATION

Before the class, find some suitable extracts 5–10 minutes in length (for example, George Winston (piano), Jean Michel Jarre (synthesizers), Weather Report (jazz), Alan Parsons Project, Vangelis, George Benson (guitar), ethnic music (Greek, Italian, Arab, Russian, Chinese, etc.), classical music, student selections, etc.).

IN CLASS

Start the music for a few minutes before the first arrival so that the students know they are entering a new and different environment as they come in; or ask the first student who arrives to start the tape-recorder.

During these first few minutes, you may want to speak to the students individually, to welcome them and get them adjusted to a new musical environment.

VARIATION

Since students may arrive at slightly different times, you could ask them to keep a class journal and write in it for the first few minutes every day. They could describe the music they hear or say what it makes them think of. Once everyone is present and has written at least one sentence, the lesson can begin. Experiment with either leaving the music on or turning it off to mark the change of tempo into another type of activity.

REMARKS

Whatever you play, at least for the first few days, should be discussed or written about so that you can judge if the music bothers anyone. Some of my students wrote that a particular kind of music prevented them from concentrating. Experiment until you find a kind of music conducive to work.

2.2   Background music

LEVEL

All levels

TIME

During regular classroom activities

AIM

To relax and/or stimulate the students while they are composing, reading, speaking in pairs, etc.

PREPARATION	None.
IN CLASS	Experiment with different types of background music to go with different types of activities. With reading and writing activities, slow music may stimulate thinking. While students are doing pair work, more lively music (cocktail-party jazz) may create a more social atmosphere in which they can interact (it might also make them speak louder and enunciate more clearly!).
VARIATION	When doing historical or topic-based activities, music of the period or geographical area may further stimulate students. For example, when studying *The Great Gatsby*, you could put on jazz music of the time. If you are discussing the conditions of blacks in the US, gospel and other forms of black music may be very suitable. When discussing the conditions of blacks in South Africa, someone like Johnny Clegg (who is actually white) may be stimulating.
REMARKS	It is always a good idea to ask students if the music bothers them, or if they like it while they are working. Volume is another factor that may please or distract students. Generally, it is best to keep it low and background.

2.3   Stop and find

LEVEL	**All levels**
TIME	**5–10 minutes** (As an ice-breaker at the beginning of a class, or as an energy-raiser during the class.)
AIM	To practise formulating closed questions (with *do* and *have*).
PREPARATION	Prepare a list of tasks that you want your students to do during the pauses in the music, such as: – *Find someone who has a pair of yellow socks.* This will elicit *Do you have . . . ?/Have you got . . . ?*, present) – *Find someone who likes Mozart.* (*Do you like . . . ?*, present/likes) – *Find someone who plays tennis.* (*Do you play . . . ?*, present/sports) – *Touch something green.* (Total Physical Response) – *Find someone who woke up late today.* (*Did you wake up . . . ?*, past) – *Find someone who has seen* (recent movie). (*Have you seen . . . ?*, present perfect)

IN CLASS

1 Explain to the students that when the music stops, you will call out an order or some instructions. The students need to follow them as quickly as possible. When the music starts again they must walk briskly around the perimeter of the class without saying anything.

2 Play some lively music and stop it every 15–20 seconds. Give each instruction loudly and clearly. Allow enough time for most but not all of the students to complete the task.

3 Start the music again.

4 Stop the activity before students get tired of it, so that you can repeat it another day.

REMARKS

This activity can, of course, be done with any kind of music, instrumental or vocal. But the music needs to be lively in order to get students moving.

Acknowledgement
I first saw this demonstrated by Anton Prochazka.

2.4   Musical reactions

LEVEL

Intermediate to advanced

TIME

Variable

AIM

To develop imaginative skills and promote discussion.

PREPARATION

1 Find one or more instrumental pieces that are not too familiar to the students.

2 Prepare a hand-out like the one below.

3 Make enough copies for everyone in the class.

IN CLASS

1 Ask students to fill out the questionnaire while listening to the music. (See Sample Hand-out.)

2 Then ask them to compare and discuss their answers with a partner.

VARIATION

1 Put up some large pictures of people at the front of the class and ask the students to match the people with the music played. Ask:
– *Who do you think will prefer what kind of music?*

2 Afterwards students compare their matchings and explain any differences.

SAMPLE HAND-OUT

---

1 If you turned on the radio and heard this piece of music would you:
   a. turn it off immediately?
   b. listen attentively?   c. buy the record?
   d. leave it on as background music   e....?

2 Imagine someone who loves this music. Describe the person in a few words.
   ....

3 Imagine someone who hates this music. Describe the person in a few words.
   ....

4 What emotions does it evoke in you?
   ....

5 What do you see if you close your eyes as you listen?
   ....

6 What nationality is the composer? From which period?
   ....

7 If this were the background music for an advertisement, what do you think the advertised product would be?
   ....

8 In what kind of place would you be most likely to hear this music?
   ....

Acknowledgement
This is an adaptation of an idea from Marianne Vaney.

2.5   My favourite moment

LEVEL   **Intermediate to advanced**

TIME   **15–30 minutes**

AIM   To practise giving descriptions, using the five senses.

PREPARATION   1 Find a dreamy piece of music to play.

2 Prepare questions to guide the students through a visualization using their senses. For example:
– *See a picture in your mind.*
– *Look at the top right-hand side of your mental picture. What is there?*
– *Look at the top left. What do you see?*
– *Now look at the middle.*
– *Notice the lighting. Where is it coming from? How bright is it?*
– *'Unfreeze' your image. What can you hear now?*
– *Can you smell anything?*
– *What can you feel with your hands, or on your skin?*
– *Are you in the picture?* etc.

IN CLASS

1 Tell students they should just relax as they listen to the music. If they wish, they can close their eyes.

2 Ask them to imagine a favourite moment in their childhood and to hold it for a moment, like a photograph in their minds. Each time you give an instruction, speak softly but clearly, and allow time between instructions for students to understand what they are supposed to do and see.

3 Ask the students the questions you have prepared.

4 After a short pause, they open their eyes and tell a partner what it was they saw, heard, smelt, felt, and tasted. Those who wish to can then share with the class their favourite moments. Replay the music in the background.

VARIATION 1

The students can describe their favourite moments in writing, and then read them to the class.

VARIATION 2

Students could draw the scene, with the text written neatly beside their pictures, to be displayed on the walls for other students to read.

VARIATION 3

You could read a student text without saying the student's name. The others can try to guess whose composition it is.

Acknowledgement
Heather Murray first showed me a variation of this activity.

2.6   Stream of consciousness writing

LEVEL

Intermediate to advanced

TIME

5–15 minutes

AIM

To encourage fluency and quantity in writing.

PREPARATION

Find a dynamic piece of music with lots of mood changes (for example, Mozart's Symphony No. 25).

IN CLASS

1 Explain to students that you are going to play a short piece of music (2–4 minutes). They are to begin writing as soon as the music starts and should not stop while the music is playing. They should not worry too much about spelling and grammar—what you want is a large amount of writing. They should write whatever comes to them.

2 When they have finished writing, students are usually interested in reading each other's work. Ask them to exchange papers and replay the music while they are reading.

VARIATION	1 You may want to give the students a subject to write about, to give them an idea: *My family, Girls and boys, Sports, War and peace, My future, A day in my life*, etc. (Or perhaps more creatively, *A day with my favourite singer, If I were president, The advantages of square potatoes or round buildings*.)

2 Stop after a few minutes, and ask the students to exchange papers and write questions for each other about what was written.

3 Then return the papers to their owners and play the tape again while they expand on what they had written, on the basis of the questions.

REMARKS

As this is a fluency exercise, you should not correct spelling and grammar, but rather comment on the amount of language produced, the quality of the images and vocabulary, and the ideas. After making positive comments on the content you might want to encourage the students to work in pairs to edit their writing and find any mistakes.

Acknowledgement
I am indebted to Anne-Christine Doebelin for this activity.

2.7 Film music

LEVEL

Intermediate to advanced

TIME

10–20 minutes

AIM

To practise *would/might*; to explore different associations with the same piece of music; and to identify musical stereotypes.

PREPARATION

1 Find some music (of any style) that is relatively unknown to the students. Tell them that this is to be the theme music for a movie or TV series.

2 Prepare a hand-out (see Sample Hand-out below) with specific questions on the music and the associations it evokes.

**SAMPLE
HAND-OUT**

---

1 Write two or three adjectives to describe the music.

2 If this music were the theme for a film or TV series, what would the film be about? (cowboy, spy, dance, police/detective, love story, soap opera, children's film, etc.)

3 Where would the action of the film take place, and in what country?

4 What would the main character be like? (male/female, profession, looks, etc.)

5 What would happen in the film?

6 How would it end?

7 What would the title be?

IN CLASS

1 Hand out the questions and make sure they are understood.

2 Play the tape as the students write their responses.

3 Then ask the students to compare what they have written with a partner.

4 Follow this up with group feedback.

VARIATION

Instead of one piece of music, you could choose several different styles of music and ask the students to make associations for each style within a grid.

EXAMPLE

Music	Place	People	Actions	Name of film
1				
2				
3				

At the end of the activity show an excerpt from the BBC programme *Music, Music, Music* to illustrate how we stereotype different types of film music (sea-adventure, cowboy, space music, etc.).

2.8 Advertising jingles

LEVEL

Upper-intermediate to advanced

TIME

45–90 minutes

AIM

To play with the language of advertising and to show the power of music accompanying a message.

PREPARATION

Record a number of short pieces of music (roughly one-third as many as there are students in your class). These might be introductions to well-known songs, lasting ten seconds or so, or they could be actual jingles or short pieces of classical music. Make sure there is a good contrast of styles and tempo.

IN CLASS

1 Ask students to number a sheet of paper from 1 to . . . (the number of pieces of music that you have). Explain to them that each person is an advertising executive with a great number of products to sell and an unlimited budget. They will listen to a number of pieces of music and decide which is right for which product. (You could first brainstorm a certain number of products on the board, or leave it to your students' imaginations.) When they hear a piece, they are to choose what they think would be an appropriate product to accompany the music in a TV advertisement.

2 Pause for a few seconds before continuing with the next piece.

3 When they have finished the activity, ask the students to compare with a partner and to see if they chose more or less the same products. Replay the music and let them discuss their choices as they hear them.

4 Next, divide the class into pairs, or small groups. Tell them they are to write a short commercial. It can be a radio or TV commercial. There should be a speaking role for each person in the group and they should really try to sell the product. The commercial should last the same time as the piece of music, or not much longer. Students can sing part of it if they want to. They will need at least fifteen minutes to write and stage it all. You will need to supply them with a copy of the tape and then provide them with cassette players, or perhaps do this in the language laboratory.

5 Allow for performance time for all the commercials. They could be spread out over one or more classes, depending on the number of students.

VARIATION 1

After the final performances, ask students to write down which advertisement they thought was the best and which products they would actually buy as a result of hearing the advertisement. Students can compare their answers and hand them in to you for *your* evaluation of the activity.

VARIATION 2

Video taping the performance is fun, and students love watching themselves. A lot of the activities done with song video clips could be done with class clips. (See Section 5.)

3 The artists and the industry

This section extends the kinds of activity already introduced in Section 1, but focuses primarily on the artists themselves and on the music industry.

The activities in this section capitalize on the widespread availability of magazine articles on these topics. Apart from the specialist magazines such as *Melody Maker*, *Smash Hits*, and *Rolling Stone*, many general interest publications, such as *Newsweek*, *Time*, and the Sunday colour supplements carry articles on music.

In countries where English language newspapers or magazines are not available, teachers fluent in the language of the country may wish to translate and adapt material written for a particular readership to the level of the students.

A number of EFL magazines publish articles geared to the lower and intermediate levels—*Speak Up* (Italy), *Spotlight* (Germany), and *I love English* (France). In addition, *Le Français dans le monde* has regular music features, while the German *Spectrum* has used songs and also developed a cassette for teachers to use in the classroom. Almost everything that is available in the United States is now also available in Japan, often with Japanese notes.

3.1   Who am I?

LEVEL
: **All levels**

TIME
: **10 minutes** (at the beginning of class, or as a break)

AIM
: To practise asking *yes/no* questions and to energize students into moving around and interacting.

PREPARATION
: Write the names of well-known singers and musicians on small pieces of paper or on Post-it pads. Make enough for all the students in your class. You may want to use the names in the hit parade, but mix them up with a few classical and 'golden oldie' names. (Mozart, Elvis Presley, Louis Armstrong, etc.)

IN CLASS
: 1 Stick a name on each student's back with sticky tape. Ensure that you put a number of female artists on the backs of male students and vice versa. The students must not see what the name is.

2 Then tell the students they can find out who they are only by asking the other students *yes/no* questions. They can only ask one question per student (thus they interact with more people). Those answering the questions can only say *yes* or *no*, or *I don't know* (if they do not know the artist). Put a label on your own back and demonstrate a few questions to get them started.
– *Am I a woman?*
– *Am I alive?*
– *Am I American?* etc.

VARIATION 1

At the end of the activity, if any students have not discovered who they are, they can come to the front of the class and tell the class all they know about themselves. The class is allowed to give them clues to help them guess.

VARIATION 2

Ask the students to write a description of themselves (from what they have learnt by asking questions), without saying who they are. Display these descriptions around the room. Students can walk around, read them, and see if they recognize them.

VARIATION 3

This activity can also be done with musical instruments (*What am I?*) or popular song titles (*Am I rock n' roll? Do I have the word 'love' in me?*).

REMARKS

This activity is great fun to do.

3.2 Sorting artists

LEVEL

All levels

TIME

5–15 minutes

AIM

To practise giving opinions; using conditionals.

PREPARATION

Beginners will need some preparation in the specific type of language used to classify and assert in a previous class: *I think . . . I would put . . . He/She belongs in this group . . . Why would you put . . . there?*

IN CLASS

1 Ask the students to form groups of four and to brainstorm the names of artists and musicians.

2 After a few minutes, ask a member from one group to write their list on the board. The other groups write up only names that are not already on the board.

3 Then ask them to work in pairs to order the names into whatever categories they see fit. Set a time limit of five minutes. (Students will usually think of the obvious categories of rock, rap, heavy

metal, country, etc. However, some students might categorize them by nationality, sex, long/short name, real/weird name, etc.)

4 After they have classified the names, ask the students to explain their categories to other pairs and to discuss the differences in their choices of categories.

VARIATION 1

You can ask students to write their groupings on a sheet of paper without giving a title to the categories. On the back of the paper they should list their categories. Display the papers around the room and ask the students to circulate and try to guess what the category headings for the groupings were. This can form the basis for later discussion on their categorizations and any inconsistencies.

VARIATION 2

The same could be done with song titles as well, either with known or unknown songs, with or without special regard to the semantic content of the songs.

REMARKS

It is important to stress to the students that no categorization is wrong, nor is any one better than another, although once set, there may be inconsistencies within categories. One of the greatest learning outcomes of such exercises is the realization that our conventions are precarious, relative, and not self-evident. You may need to tell the students repeatedly that there is no one right way to do this kind of activity, nor is there one right answer.

Acknowledgement
Simone Dévéreaz first showed me how to do this.

3.3   Proximity genre map

LEVEL

Intermediate to advanced

TIME

10–20 minutes

AIM

To practise the language of agreement, disagreement, and compromise.

PREPARATION

Make a list of all the different names of musical genres (opera, rock, blues, soul, folk, etc.).

IN CLASS

1 Ask students individually to list all the types (genres) of music they can think of. Explain the word 'genre' if you intend to use it.

2 Students form small groups of five or six and combine their lists.

3 Ask a member from each group to write up their list of genres on the board.

4 Then ask all the students to put the names on the blackboard into a proximity-relationship network (see example below). Some might put country and classical very far apart on their sheet of paper, with opera probably closer to classical, and blues closer to country. If they have never heard of a style of music they should leave it out or ask a friend. (There will probably be new ones for you, too.)

EXAMPLE

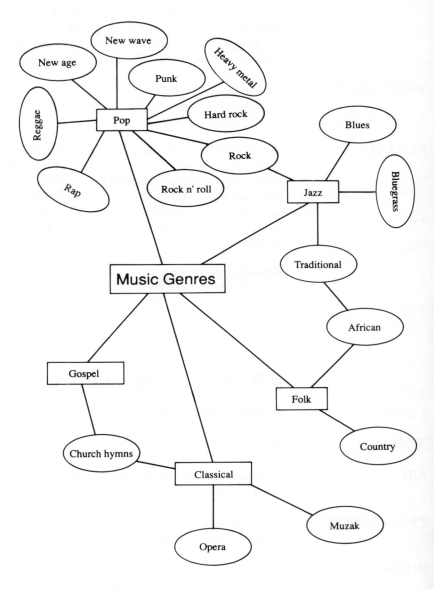

5 When they have completed their genre map, they should compare it with others in small groups and try to account for their positionings.

VARIATION

In groups of four, students pass their papers one-to-the-right and write a sentence of disagreement at the bottom of each paper, for example, *I don't think rock n' roll and gospel should be so close together.* After the papers have been around the four-person groups, each person tries to justify their genre map, agreeing or disagreeing with the comments that were made about it. (Allow fifteen minutes for this variation.)

REMARKS

Because many students have in-depth knowledge of certain genres, they usually end up teaching the others about it, as they explain why two genres might be interrelated. This gives you the opportunity to fade into the background and move into a learning mode. You will find your 'letting go' will encourage interaction and productive use of language among the students.

3.4   Identity cards

LEVEL

False beginners to advanced

TIME

60 minutes (or several 20-minute sessions)

AIM

To practise all forms of questions.

PREPARATION

1 Find a pop star profile in one of the music magazines (see the Sample Profile at the end of the activity) and make sure you have enough copies for the students.

2 Prepare a set of questions from the information in the profile.

IN CLASS

False beginners

1 Hand out copies of the profile and write one question on the board at a time, for example:
– *What is the star's family name?*
– *What does he/she like?*

2 After the students have found the answers from the profile in front of them, write a longer set of questions on the board for the students to answer. Ask them to compare their answers with their partner's. When they have finished, ask for the answers and write them on the board beside the questions.

3 Then single out one of the students and ask the rest of the class the same questions:
– *What is his/her name?*
Erase the earlier answers on the board as you do this and write up the new answers.

4 Ask each student to write a personal identity card with all the information except their names.

EXAMPLE

Name	Preferred music ....
First name	A favourite film ....
Date of birth	A favourite book ....
Place of birth	Hobbies ....
Astrological birth sign	Loves ....
Height	Hates ....
Eye colour	Hopes for the future ....
Hair colour	

5 When they have done this, collect the cards and redistribute them at random and ask students to find the person who wrote the card by going round asking *yes/no* questions (demonstrate this once if necessary). When they have found all the card owners, they sit down and write a composition about the person.

Intermediate to advanced
1 Ask students to write down the questions needed to get information about a star from looking at a sample identity card. They then ask a partner their questions. The partner responds with information from the identity card.

2 Next, students make their own identity card for themselves.

3 In pairs, they then ask the relevant questions of each other.

VARIATION 1

Pairs fill out an identity card for each other asking the appropriate questions, as if in an interview situation.

VARIATION 2

The activity can be extended with a *He/She loves . . .* and *He/She hates . . .* list.

VARIATION 3

More advanced students can expand the interview questions further in a role-play and/or a written description.

VARIATION 4

Finally, using the information in the profile, stage a mock radio or video programme in which students conduct an interview, with someone acting as a pop star.

Acknowledgement
I am indebted to Simone Dévéreaz for this activity.

PROFILE: MADONNA

Full name Blanche Madonna
Louise Ciccone
Date of birth 15 August 1959
Place of birth Bay City
Height 1.62m
Weight 53kg

A born winner

Blanche Madonna Louise Ciccone was
the third of eight children. Her mother
died when she was six, and from then on
she had to help her Italian father to
bring up her younger brothers and
sisters.

Although her father was very strict and
disapproved of her studying modern
dance at the University of Michigan,
Madonna had already decided on her
career as a performer, and nothing was
going to stop her.

In the 1970s she worked for a while in
Paris, but soon decided New York was
the place for her. Soon the whole of

New York showbiz agreed with her, and
she was destined for success.

World records

By 1984, Madonna had sold 3.5 million
records of *Like A Virgin*, and had
appeared on 117 magazine covers
around the world.

Unusal star

In 1985 two things happened: she
married actor Sean Penn, and she
appeared in *Desperately Seeking Susan*.
In it, she played someone very like
herself. In *Shanghai Surprise* she
played a very different sort of role – that
of a missionary.

At the same time as filming, Madonna
was producing her third album, *True
Blue*.

Madonna has often been at the centre of
controversy. Some say she is only
interested in making money – she says
all she wants is love. What is certain is
that she is bright, beautiful, and highly
talented.

3.5   Magazine interview

LEVEL   **Intermediate to advanced**

TIME   **15 minutes**

AIM   To formulate open-ended questions from given answers.

PREPARATION   1 Find an interview with a pop star in a music magazine (see the
example below).

2 Type out the answers, leaving blanks for the questions. Make
copies for the whole class.

IN CLASS   1 In class, go over the answers to make sure they are understood.

2 Ask students to formulate the questions that would get the
answers in the interview.

3 When they have finished, ask the students to compare with a
partner to see if they agree.

4 Then ask for volunteers to put the questions up on the board.

VARIATION   Students can later act out the interview, ad-libbing as they like.

SAMPLE
INTERVIEW

Interviewer ...?
A Well my family is rather boring, actually.
Interviewer ...
A My father's a lawyer and my mother a housewife.
Interviewer ...?
A No, I'm an only child.
Interviewer ...?
A Well, being alone a lot, I had to make up my own games. I had a lot of conversations with myself and started writing them down when I was eight or nine. Songwriting just kind of came out of that.
Interviewer ...?
A No, I don't really like touring. I prefer working in the studio and writing new songs.
Interviewer ...?
A I guess Simon and Garfunkel had the biggest influence on me when I was growng up. But lately I'm more into jazz.

REMARKS   If you are unable to find an interview, make one up from an informative article. In either case, keep it short!

Acknowledgement
I first saw this activity described by Jane Myles in *Catch* No 2 Oct-Nov 1985.

3.6   Role-play interview

LEVEL   **Intermediate to advanced**

TIME   **10–15 minutes**

AIM   To practise asking questions, and role-playing.

PREPARATION   None.

IN CLASS   1 Ask students to pretend that they are journalists and that they will be interviewing a singer that you have recently talked about or whose song you have just heard.

2 They each write three questions they would like to ask this artist, about his or her personal or professional life.

3 When they have completed this, ask for a volunteer to play the role of the artist. The volunteer goes to the front of the class and answers the other students' questions. Encourage this student to enter into the personality of the artist. It may help to take him or her out of the class for a moment to prepare for the role.

VARIATION 1   If you do not have an extrovert performer in your class, ask the students to do the role-play in pairs. Each partner takes turns at acting out the artist.

VARIATION 2   Another option for pairs is to let them exchange their questions and to write creative responses to them, and then to act out the dialogues in small groups.

REMARKS   1 Activity 3.5 is a good lead-in to this activity.

2 It is important to bear in mind that such role-plays and 'exposed' activities only work really well when you have already established a trusting and non-threatening environment in the classroom.

3.7   Pop group interview

LEVEL   Intermediate to advanced

TIME   40 minutes

AIM   To develop interviewing skills, through role-play and acting.

PREPARATION   Prepare copies of the sample forms below.

IN CLASS   1 Ask four students to volunteer to be members of a pop group. The rest of the class will be music journalists. While the pop group fill out a press release for themselves (Form 1), the journalists, in groups of four to six, decide which magazine they are writing for, who their target audience is, and what they are interested in.

2 When the pop group has finished the press releases, they keep one for reference and give three to the journalists for them to write questions they would like to ask the group. While the journalists are writing questions, members of the pop group fill out individual life history forms (Form 2).

3 Stage a press conference with you as the PR manager for the group. The group members take turns at answering the journalists' questions.

SAMPLE PRESS RELEASE

Press release

- Name of group ....
- Manager's name ....
- Members' names ....
- Length of time together ....
- Record contract with ....

- Touring schedule for the next four months ....
- Most recent record release ....
- Style of music ....
- Short historical sketch ....
- Recent developments and future plans ....

SAMPLE BIOGRAPHY

Individual biography

- Real name . . . .
- Age . . . .
- Previous bands . . . .
- Since . . . .
- Songwriting? . . . .
- Hobbies . . . .
- Hates . . . .

- Stage name . . . .
- Originally from . . . .
- Present band . . . .
- Instrument played . . . .
- Distinguishing characteristics . . . .
- Loves . . . .
- Style of dress . . . .

Acknowledgement
This is a version of an idea from Peter Watcyn-Jones I saw in *Act English*, 1985.

3.8   Musical words list

LEVEL

All levels

TIME

15 minutes

AIM

To make students aware of how much English musical terminology exists in their own language.

PREPARATION

Ask the students to bring in some music magazines in their own language, or you could record a pop music programme, especially one in which the disc jockey talks a lot.

IN CLASS

1 Ask the students to look at the magazines or let them listen to a tape of disc-jockey talk. Ask them to write down all the English words that are used.

2 Ask them to add to this list any other English words that are regularly used in their language when talking about music.

3 When they have finished their lists, ask them to compare them with a partner to see what they might have missed, and to discuss any differences. Finally, write the list on the board from students' dictation. Allow time for small group or whole class discussion of their meanings if need be.

VARIATION 1   More advanced students try to embed all the terms into English sentences, or write an article including them.

VARIATION 2   Ask the students to think of a desirable T-shirt text or slogan using some of the words.

REMARKS   Try to see this activity as a learning experience for you. Note that the jargon of pop music changes very rapidly. Vocabulary in fashion five to ten years ago may now be obsolete. Be on guard for words that may have changed meaning from one language to other (false friends). This activity may be easier with certain languages that borrow heavily and easily from English. With some language groups it may be too unrealistic to attempt.

3.9   Music journal

LEVEL   All levels

TIME   5 minutes a day

AIM   To encourage fluency in written work.

PREPARATION   Prepare a hand-out similar to the one in the example below.

SAMPLE HAND-OUT

Your music journal

Every day you will write for five minutes in your music journal. You can describe the music that is being played, give your opinion of it, tell what you know about the artist(s), and/or simply say what it makes you think of. Try not to be too concerned about correct grammar and spelling. The important thing is to write a lot. For example, you might write something like:

This music sounds like rock. The singer's voice is rough and the electric guitars are screaming. The artist is Bruce Springsteen, I think. The picture on the board looks like Rambo. Now the song has changed and the song is much softer. I like the song but I don't understand the lyrics very much. I would like to read them if possible (the soft one). It makes me think of a concert I went to once with my best friend. It was summertime ...

IN CLASS   This can be done for the first few minutes of each class as the students arrive. They write a journal (in a special notebook set aside for this purpose) about the music that is playing. They describe the music, give their opinions of it, or simply write how they feel about it, letting their minds wander with the music. The important thing is that they should write whatever comes into their minds. (See also activities 2.1 and 2.4.)

VARIATION 1   Students can do this as homework five minutes a day and hand in their notebooks to you every week or two.

VARIATION 2   Students may want to share their journals with others and let them read what they have written.

VARIATION 3   Pictures of the artist, which the students can also write about, can be displayed with each different musical selection.

VARIATION 4   Experiment with the journals for two weeks. Then stop the activity for a week or two and discuss it with the class. Ask the students what they thought of it and what they felt they had been learning/practising.

VARIATION 5   Periodically, do some feedback work with vocabulary and expressions that students have been using, getting wrong, or that they might need in the future. Right and wrong phrases can be mixed up. The students work in pairs to decide which are wrong and how they might be corrected. You may want to follow this up with a journal feedback form (see example below).

EXAMPLE

Journal feedback

The following expressions caused some problems in the journals over the last few weeks.

1 We *hear* music, but we *listen to* music.
2 *It remembers me* should be *It reminds me of ...*
3 When you say *I can't hear the words*, you probably want to say *I can't understand the words* or *I can't catch the words* (which implies you cannot hear them well enough to understand them) or *The music drowns the words*.
4 *Old fashioned* means that it is not *current* or *modern*; *old people's music* sounds rather like an insult towards older people! Words to try to use in the next few weeks:
   • *melody   melodious*
   • *harmony   harmonious*
   • *a good beat*
   • *mysterious*
   • *'the look'*
   • *looks like*

REMARKS   This is a fluency activity. The important thing is for students to write a lot. They will stop writing a lot if you correct them too much and fail to give positive feedback on quantity, creativity, etc. After correcting the grammar, spelling, style, etc., be sure to make a positive comment about how well the students have done!

3.10   Hit chart: story writing

LEVEL   Intermediate to advanced

TIME   10–30 minutes

AIM   To practise using idiomatic phrases in context.

PREPARATION
1 You can use the chart in activity 1.4 or any other that you find.
2 Make sure there are enough copies for the whole class.

IN CLASS
1 Go over the song titles with students to check comprehension. Explain any ambiguity and ask a few questions:
– *She Drives me Crazy: Is this good or bad?*
Conduct short discussions about the titles when appropriate:
– *Beauty's Only Skin Deep: Do you believe it? Have you ever known someone like that?*

2 Ask the students to write a short story incorporating as many of the song titles as they can. Demonstrate orally how they might do this:
Looking at the world outside my window one day I saw someone who was like a prayer. And now she drives me crazy every time I see her.

3 Explain to the students that they have the right to use poetic licence and to change the pronouns and verb tenses to fit their narratives.

VARIATION 1   As a warm-up with advanced students, you might like to ask them to do this activity orally in pairs first, taking turns putting song titles into a context they construct as they go along. (This usually leads to much laughter!)

VARIATION 2   Students can work in pairs to write down phrases, competing against each other. Set a time limit of 30 seconds per sentence. The partners then read each other's phrases and ask you to arbitrate on the best.

VARIATION 3   If the students feel comfortable about reading each other's stories out loud, it is usually a lot of fun and reinforces the meanings of the idiomatic phrases.

VARIATION 4   Another possibility is to ask the students to write a dialogue (for example, two lovers talking) in pairs, using the song titles. The partners then perform the dialogue for the class, possibly even video-taping them.

VARIATION 5   If no hit chart is available, make the class's own as in 1.11.

3.11   Hit chart: discussion

LEVEL

Intermediate to advanced

TIME

15–30 minutes

AIM

To develop a critical awareness of the music industry. To encourage fluency in discussion.

PREPARATION

1 Try to obtain a musical chart, preferably an airplay chart. (See activity 1.4.)

2 Prepare a list of questions on a hand-out. For example:

SAMPLE HAND-OUT

---

1 Does the chart tell you what has been played the most, or sold the most records, or advertised the most?

2 Does it show what is best? What do we mean by 'best'?

3 How many of these songs have you:
   • heard?
   • seen on video clips?
   • taped from radio or from your friends?
   • bought?

4 When you buy new songs, what influences you most:
   • the opinion of your friends?
   • the opinion of your family?

   • the fact that you have heard them on the radio or TV?
   • the fact that they are high in the charts?
   • other?

5 Do people buy songs because they hear them on the radio? Or does the radio play songs because many people have bought them?

6 What are the factors which help a song rise quickly in the charts?

7 Are there any songs you feel should be included in the chart but which are not there?

IN CLASS

1 Students work in pairs to discuss the questions on the hand-out.

2 When they have finished, one student acts as 'chairperson', collecting feedback from all the other pairs.

3 You, the teacher, should stay in the background.

REMARKS

Charts can be chosen not only for pop music but also for folk, classical, regional/national music, etc.

3.12 Pop songs: discussion

LEVEL   Intermediate to advanced

TIME   Variable

AIM   To encourage fluency.

PREPARATION   1 Find a number of songs which students already know and which have themes and topics suitable for class discussion. (There is a list of themes and songs in the Appendix.) Alternatively, use songs which you have already exploited in other ways.

2 Make copies of the lyrics.

3 List possible discussion questions. These should not have definite answers in the text nor be simply what you want to hear. They should be issues you would naturally discuss with your own acquaintances, things that you wonder about yourself.

IN CLASS   1 Ask small groups or pairs of students to read the lyrics of a song and make up discussion questions based upon the song or arising from its main themes.

2 Ask each group to write their three best questions up on the board. As they do so, note the similarities and differences in the questions from the different groups.

3 Finally, ask the students to form new groups to discuss the questions they find most interesting. (See the list of songs and their thematic categories in the Appendix. Some are 'engaged' songs about social issues, and others are more personal songs.) Either type can spark off different type of discussion.

VARIATION   This activity can be extended into compostion. Ask students to write about the question they found most stimulating.

3.13 Pop industry: discussion

LEVEL   Intermediate to advanced

TIME   Variable

AIM   To encourage fluency and to make students aware of the many aspects of the pop industry and the way it works.

PREPARATION
1 Find a suitable article, pop star profile, or extract from a newspaper or magazine about a recent concert or music topic. (See Sample Materials below or the Bibliography for a list of suggested sources.) Concerts for Amnesty International or other sponsored charity events usually lead to a number of published articles.

2 Ensure you have enough copies for the whole class.

IN CLASS
1 Hand out copies of the article (with photos if possible).

2 Then carry out any of the following procedures:
a. Explain the general topic, but put up on the board a few questions you would like the students to find answers for. For example:
- *How does the music industry work? Who gets the money?*
- *What effect does pirating have on the industry?*
- *What effect does music have (physically, emotionally, and socially) on us?*
- *How do you feel about pop stars in advertising?*
- *What do you think about music for fund raising?*

b. Ask the students to read the article in pairs and discuss.
c. Students read the article and make up questions for others to answer.
d. Students underline the parts they do not quite understand or would like you to expand on.

SAMPLE MATERIALS 1

Voices: What do you think about the music kids are listening to today?

Billy Williams, 58
Assistant Principal
Oak Ridge, Tenn.
As a parent, I would be more cautious about the kind of music they are listening to. I was never too concerned about the music my kids listened to in the mid-'60s and '70s, and I wish I had been. If there's nothing but a color code, music should labeled to warn parents about what they purchase for minors.

Gloria Jean Barber, 47
Secretary
Vancouver, Wash.
On the whole, I don't think it's bad. I'm not into heavy rock, but most of the music is no worse than what I listened to when I was growing up. As a matter of fact, I heard some of the same complaints. I don't see any sense in warning labels on records because who reads labels anyway? Few people do.

Willa Mae Cochran, 64
Homemaker
Columbus, Ohio
Some of the music is immoral. Kids should be listening to sensible music with messages like staying away from drugs or staying in school. There are some rap songs that are all right. But all this sexual stuff is not good. Songs can have a beat that kids can dance to without all the profanity.

Carol Schibi, 39
Networking coordinator
Pilot Grove, Mo.
I have three teenagers and, overall, they have good music. We've discussed Guns 'N' Roses, and we don't play that type of music in the house. I don't think that banning music is the answer, but parents have to be responsible for what their children listen to. I don't see anything wrong with rating music.

Michael Phillips, 17
Student/studio musician
Mount Vermont, N. Y.
I like music a lot – the harmonies and the way it's played. But I'm really interested in jazz. Everything comes from jazz. There is a lot of negative music out there, and if people listen to it enough, it sticks in your head and brings out the negative side in you. I think there should be warning labels on some of the songs.

Shawn Mulhern, 49
Radio personality
Green Bay, Wis.
The music is probably way too violent. And it doesn't make a whole lot of sense as far as the lyrics are concerned. If it doesn't damage your mind, it certainly would damage your ears. I have respect for anybody's music. But it just seems that there's never any end to how far record producers want to take it.

**SAMPLE
MATERIALS 2**

Pop Lyrics: A Mirror and a Molder of Society

Sheila Davis

In the thirty-one years since *Et Cetera* published S.I. Hayakawa's paper 'Popular Songs vs. the Facts of Life' assessing the 'underlying orientations, and implied attitudes' reflected in pop lyrics, major social forces have combined to reshape the sound and the content of our songs – the Sexual Revolution; the Women's Movement; the dominance in the recording marketplace by the creative hyphenate (the singer-songwriter-arranger-producer), and the growing 'africanisation' of American music. If Dr Hayakawa were listening to top-40 radio today, he would hear a radical change in both the attitudes and the language of popular songs.

For one thing, the belief in magic, miracles, and a love to last forever – manifest in so many pre-rock era songs – is expressed only occasionally in contemporary lyrics. Lionel Richie would seem to be the last bastion of romanticism, still proclaiming the viability of 'Endless Love', and affecting an open-hearted vulnerability in 'Truly' and 'Still'. Today long-term interpersonal relationships are more generally viewed as difficult, if not impossible, as in such hits as 'Hard Time for Lovers' and 'What's Forever For?'. In spite of an occasional 'we can work it out' sentiment, the overriding emotion is disillusionment, reflecting the current one-out-of-three divorce rate.

Female passivity, like commitment, is out of style. The lyrical wimp, who Hayakawa heard whining in 'Can't Help Lovin' Dat Man', has been replaced with the EST-inspired assertiveness of such female anthems as 'I Will Survive' and 'It's My Turn'.

VARIATION 1

1 If you were to use Sample Materials 1, ask the students to read through the different opinions and simply note down whether they are positive or negative, and then list them from most positive to most negative. (If they do not understand a word or phrase, they ask their partner or you.)

2 Students compare their lists in pairs and discuss any discrepancies.

3 Still in pairs, students work to list all the reasons why these people think we should or should not put labels on records.

4 Ask the pairs to think of any other reasons for or against labelling (the right to free speech, for instance).

5 Students then write a passage about the same length as one of the magazine quotations, using what they think are the most important arguments presented, together with their own.

6 Form small groups in which students read each others' texts.

7 You could further extend this variation by asking the students to pick one of the characters in the magazine texts to elaborate on. (What kind of person do they think he/she is, what are his/her hobbies, politics? etc.)

8 Another possibility is to let the small groups role-play the people in the article.

VARIATION 2

1 With Sample Materials 2, you might give the following background information to help the students to understand the article:

> In 1954, a man named Hayakawa wrote a paper describing pop songs. He said they reflected the theme of 'love forever' as in a fairy tale. Apparently in the 1960s and 1970s songs changed a bit and love forever was not always the message. Instead, 'a good time for a night' was OK and songs became more 'sexplicit'. This article raises the question of whether songs describe what society is doing, or whether they provoke society into action. The same questions holds for violence on TV. 'Is it an accurate reflection of reality? Does showing provoke more of it?'

2 Ask students to read the extracts and then to discuss in small groups. They should elect a spokesperson to summarize what the group thought.

3 Then ask them to write a composition on the theme of mirror versus moulder for homework, with examples from their own experience to support their point of view.

3.14   Song dependency

LEVEL

Advanced

TIME

20–50 minutes

AIM

To make students aware of the importance of music in their daily lives.

PREPARATION

1 Choose a literary or other text whose topic is music or song. (A good example is the sample text below.)

2 Make sure you have enough copies for everyone in the class.

IN CLASS

1 Distribute the text and ask the students to read it.

2 Discuss any conceptual or vocabulary difficulties with the students.

3 Ask the students to work in pairs to think about and discuss the following questions.
- *What do you use music for?*
- *Do you ever have songs or music running through your head? If so, what does it tell you about yourself?*
- *What can you not do without music (or not do as well)?*
- *What would the following be like without music: dancing/films/ parties/pop stars/a Walkman/saying the alphabet?*

SAMPLE TEXT

Dr P. was a musician of distinction, well-known for many years as a singer, and then, at the local School of Music, as a teacher. It was here, in relation to his students, that certain strange problems were first observed. Sometimes a student would present himself, and Dr P. would not recognize him; or, specifically, would not recognize his face. The moment the student spoke, he would be recognized by his voice. Such incidents multiplied, causing embarrassment, perplexity, fear – and, sometimes, comedy. For not only did Dr P. increasingly fail to see faces, but he saw faces when there were no faces to see: genially, Magoo-like, when in the street, he might pat the heads of water-hydrants and parking-meters, taking these to be the heads of children; he would amiably address carved knobs on the furniture, and be astounded when they did not reply. ...
How does he do anything, I wondered to myself? What happens when he's dressing, goes to the lavatory, has a bath? ... [I asked his wife] how for instance, he managed to dress himself. 'It's just like eating,' she explained. 'I put his usual clothes out, in all the usual places, and he dresses without difficulty, singing to himself. He does everything singing to himself. But if he is interrupted and loses the thread, he comes to a complete stop, doesn't know his clothes – or his own body. He sings all the time – eating songs, dressing songs, bathing songs, everything. He can't do anything unless he makes it a song'.

(Oliver Sachs: *The Man who Mistook his Wife for a Hat*)

VARIATION

Some classes might like to try making up songs such as they would sing or hum while carrying out everyday activities (like Dr P!).

3.15   Working with quotations

LEVEL

Intermediate to advanced

TIME

Variable

AIM

To stimulate discussion and composition skills.

PREPARATION

1 Collect quotations on the subject of music and song. Try to find quotations that are provocative and relevant in some way to language learners and to the interests of your students.

2 Make copies of your quotations.

3 Cut your sheet of quotations into strips, one quotation per strip.

IN CLASS

1 Ask students to work in pairs. Hand out one quotation per pair.

2 Pairs discuss their quotation for five to six minutes.

3 Each pair then writes a short summary of their discussion, including their reactions to the quotation. These compositions can be displayed in the classroom to stimulate class discussion during a later lesson.

VARIATION 1

As a warm-up, at the beginning of a class write one quotation on the board to stimulate five minutes' journal writing.

VARIATION 2

From your stock of quotations, each student chooses one to memorize and recite at an oral exam. The students have to explain why they chose that quotation, and what it means to them.

SAMPLE QUOTATIONS

1 Give me a laundry list and I'll set it to music.
(Rossini)

2 Hell is full of musical amateurs: music is the brandy of the damned.
(G.B. Shaw)

3 Music begins to atrophy when it departs too far from the dance; . . . poetry begins to atrophy when it gets too far from music.
(Ezra Pound)

4 He that lives in hope dances without music.
(George Herbert)

5 Music is essentially useless, as life is: but both lend utility to their conditions.
(George Santayana)

6 Our sweetest songs are those that tell of saddest thought.
(Shelley)

REMARKS

A good source of quotations on music and song is the *Oxford Dictionary of Quotations*.

3.16   Song titles: grammar focus

LEVEL

Intermediate to advanced

TIME

10–30 minutes

AIM

To practise identifying grammatical categories and to recognize ambiguity and the fact that words can sometimes fall into several grammatical categories.

PREPARATION

Go through the titles in a hit list (see 1.4, 1.11, 3.10, or 3.11) and think of categories you wish to ask students to identify.

IN CLASS

Ask students to count how many song titles from a hit list might fall into the grammatical categories you have chosen to look at. Below are some of the categories you might choose:

Example of categories

– *How many titles have one word? Two words?*
– *How many titles are complete sentences (imperatives or noun-verb-objects)?*
– *Are there any conditionals?*
– *How many titles are prepositional phrases/adjective+ noun clauses/in a foreign language?*
– *What is the ratio of articles to adjectives to prepositions to nouns?*
– *How many titles have words that could be verbs or nouns (e.g. 'help' or 'stop')?*
– *How many have proper names of people or places?*

(The charts you choose will often suggest other categories that you can ask for.)

4 Using songs

'What do you do with a song besides listen to it and possibly sing with it?' was the question I was asked at a presentation on pop songs in Holland in 1983. My presentation was on the conversational and 'motherese' qualities of pop songs—rather theoretical. The question pulled me back to the practical concerns of teachers. Since then, I have been collecting ideas, and the number of possibilities seem infinite to me. Again, I cannot emphasize enough that whatever you can do with a text, recording, or film, you can probably do with songs—in addition, of course, to singing!

This section looks at how the music and the lyrics of songs can be used in a classroom or language laboratory. Although it is difficult and rather unnatural to take the activities of this section and separate them into conventional skills categories of reading, writing, speaking, and listening, since we often exercise several of these skills at once, the activities in this section have been divided for the sake of convenience into two categories.

1 those which start with reading and writing and move on to listening or singing, and

2 those activites which start with listening, speaking, and singing, and then proceed to reading and writing.

The last four activities in this section were devised for use in the language laboratory. Many of the other activities could also, of course, be done in a language lab.

4.1   Text completion and construction

LEVEL

All levels

TIME

5–15 minutes

AIM

To improve listening comprehension, reading, guessing, and composition skills.

PREPARATION

1 Choose a song appropriate to the language level of the class.

2 Find a recording of it and type out the lyrics, leaving out some words or phrases. Try to space out the blanks in order to give students time to fill them in. You can, if you wish, focus on a particular word-class (verbs, prepositions, adjectives, etc.).

IN CLASS	**1** Distribute copies of the song with blanks. Students work in pairs. They first read the text together for overall comprehension, trying to think of words which might fit the blanks. (Explain any words they do not know.)
	2 Then play the recording, asking the students to fill in the missing words.
	3 Finally, ask them to tell you their answers. If there is disagreement or doubt over a given word or phrase, simply play that section of the tape again until the doubt or disagreement is resolved.
VARIATION 1	With lower-level classes, you can include a glossary of the missing words at the bottom of your typed hand-outs. The glossary might contain only the missing words, or a selection of other words to choose from.
VARIATION 2	You could leave the same number of dashes as there are letters in the missing words, and make it easier for lower-level classes by putting in the first letter. Or you could leave out more than one word, especially for idiomatic expressions, and put a number in brackets to let students know how many words are missing.
VARIATION 3	With intermediate classes the rhyming words (or just one of a pair) can be left out at the end of each line in some songs and these words guessed at from the context. It helps if you first give the rhyme scheme. (See Tilaka Sekara 1985.)
VARIATION 4	Depending on the level of the class, you could delete every fifth, seventh, or ninth word. (This is easily done on a word processor.)
VARIATION 5	When preparing the hand-outs you could insert an extra word here or there, instead of leaving words out. The task then is for the students to cross out any words that they do not hear (Davy 1985). Another possibility is to type into your hand-out lyrics which differ from those in the recording (for example, using full forms *is not* when the recorded version has *isn't* or *ain't*).
VARIATION 6	Lander (1988) suggests typing out words with mistakes in rhyme to see if the students can catch them. For example, for the song 'Land of hope and glory', he wrote 'Land of soap and glory . . . we exalt thee, who are torn of thee.' (See my version of *Groovy Kind of Love* in the example opposite.)

EXAMPLE

A friend of mine typed these lyrics for me, but
I am not sure if they are all correct. First
read through the song and underline the words
you think might be wrong. Then listen to the
song and correct any mistakes.

Gruesome Kind of Love **sung by Filcalluns**

When I'm fearing you, all I have to do
Is take a look at you, then I'm naughty glue
When you're cross with me, I can feel your
heart eat
I can hear your breathing in my hear.

Wouldn't you agree, baby, you and me got a
gruesome kind of rub?

Anytime you want to, you can turn neon to
Anything you want to, anytime a star
When I kiss your slips, oohh I start to differ
Can't control the slivering to lie.

Wouldn't you agree, baby, you and me got a
gruesome kind of rub?

When I'm fearing you, all I have to do
Is take a look at you, then I'm naughty glue
When I'm in your harm, nothing seems to
splatter
My whole world could clatter, I don't care.

Wouldn't you agree, baby, you and me got a
gruesome kind of rub?
We got a gruesome kind of love
We got a gruesome kind of love
We got a gruesome kind of love.

VARIATION 7

Selective listening can also be done without the support of the
written text. Students can listen for certain phrases, grammatical
constructions, or words, and count the number of times they occur.
This is something even beginners can do to get them to focus on
certain sounds and phrases and pick them out of a stream of speech
(Lander 1988). In addition they could number the items in the
order that they hear them (Ryding 1985).

VARIATION 8

Another option is to pre-teach words and expressions that students will hear in a song.

1 Give the students the words in random order on the blackboard or on a hand-out.

2 Tell them that the words tell a story or describe a situation and that they should first try to imagine a story of their own using the words. They either write it or tell it to a partner.

3 Next, tell the story or situation of the song and then play the song.

4 The students can then retell the story afterwards to each other in pairs. For example, from the *Streets of London*:

Acknowledgement
I am indebted to Melody Noll for this variation.

VARIATION 9

There is also great potential for photocopying errors and spilled white-out! You can delete the first or last few letters of every line, or just draw a straight or zig-zag line down the middle with white-out paint. (Of course you should excuse yourself to your students on the ground that the photocopier is acting up again!) This is a quick and easy way to make a completion exercise that is both fun and interesting. Make sure you give the students time to guess the missing letters before they listen to the song.

VARIATION 10

With advanced students, hand out your incomplete text, together with a glossary that contains not only the missing words, but a selection of synonyms as well. Students can discuss the poetic merit of each synonym before finalizing their choice.

REMARKS

1 At the beginning of the activity when students are trying to guess what might go in a blank, or making up a story, anything that is grammatically correct and possible is acceptable. Doing a gap-fill exercise is not very communicative. However, asking the students to guess at missing words from what they have understood, or creating stories demands much more language processing than simply listening and filling in.

2 Use the pause button on your tape-recorder to allow students to write difficult words.

3 Finally, there will be some times when even you do not understand all the words in a song. Let the students know you are unsure—it is reassuring for them, and may lead to an interesting discussion as to whether the words are important in the first place.

4.2 Jumbled lyrics

LEVEL — **All levels**

TIME — **15–30 minutes**

AIM — To practise listening comprehension and to encourage students to use contextual clues to order a text.

PREPARATION — 1 Choose a song, preferably one with a narrative that tells a story, and which is appropriate to the language level of your class. The song could be one contributed by a student. (See activity 1.10.)

2 Find a recording of it and type out the lyrics.

3 At this point you have two choices:
a. Make copies of the lyrics and then cut each line or verse in half horizontally or vertically, depending on the level of difficulty required, and place each cut-up whole song in an envelope.
b. Re-type the song with the sentences in a different order—either whole sentences, stanzas, or even half sentences (see example below), and make copies for the class.

IN CLASS — 1 Distribute the envelopes or photocopies to pairs and ask them to try to put the words into the correct order, depending on what they think would be a logical order. When you think that they have re-ordered some or all of it, pairs can compare their orders with other pairs.

2 Then play the recording of the song, but stop after every second line or so, for students to check their versions and to guess at what will come next.

3 Finally, listen to the whole song and discuss further amendments.

VARIATION 1 — This activity can be done with stanzas for less advanced students, or with words within lines. The same song can be used to produce a variety of graded worksheets for different levels.

VARIATION 2 — 1 Give each student a word, expression, or line of the song to listen for. (You will have to work this out on the length of the song and the number of students you have!)

2 Play the tape. As the students listen they have to arrange themselves physically in the order in which they hear their word, expression, etc.

VARIATION 3 — Advanced students working in small groups can each be given a line from a verse and asked to arrange themselves physically in the order in which they think they will be before they hear the song.

REMARKS

A wordprocessor makes the preparation of worksheets easier. During the class, if you notice you have overestimated the students' level, provide them with clues, give them the first and last sentence, use the pause button often, etc.

Acknowledgement

I first saw this activity proposed for use with songs by Reeve and Williamson (1987) in *Modern English Teacher*.

4.3   Writing to known tunes

LEVEL

Adaptable to all levels

TIME

15–40 minutes

AIM

To use language creatively and to explore the use of rhythm, rhyme, and resonance.

PREPARATION

1 Choose two or three well-known songs (such as *Jingle Bells, My Bonny Lies Over the Ocean, La Cucaracha, We Shall Overcome, Swing Low Sweet Chariot, Frère Jacques, Sur le Pont d'Avignon,* etc.). They should be simple songs with a contagious 'hummability'. If you are working with teenagers, choose current hits.

2 Type out the words of one verse and the chorus.

3 Make enough copies of your typed-up verse for everyone in the class.

IN CLASS

1 Ask the students to supply different lyrics, telling a story or describing a particular situation. This can be made easier if you give the students a theme (for example, getting up in the morning; going to bed at night; school dances; a satirical political song about a president or prime minister, describing the economic situation, etc.). The success of the exercise depends a great deal on choosing suitable subjects which encourage the students to express themselves.

2 Students should work individually at first, making a rough draft.

3 Next, they can sing their songs to each other in pairs or small groups. (If one person really cannot sing a tune, another in the group might be prepared to sing their song for them.)

4 Check at this point that the word–tune ratio is approximately right. Welcome any suggestions from other students for improvement and expansion.

5 After redrafting their songs, students can sing theirs for the entire class, either individually or in groups.

VARIATION	Give the students incomplete verses, in which they have to finish the lines or make up whole new lines.
REMARKS	A number of books give examples of popular folk and traditional tunes rewritten using conversational English suitable for beginner and intermediate levels (see Bibliography). However, when the students themselves create the lyrics, the activity is more personal and more communicative.
EXAMPLE	

• •

To the tune of *Jingle Bells*, for seven-to ten-year-olds (Juniors) in a summer sports camp.

Chorus:
Junior boys, Junior girls, laughing all the way,
Oh what fun it is to run in
Summer Camp each day.
Junior boys, Junior girls, laughing all the way,
Oh what fun it is to run the
Junior Bells all say.

We come from everywhere,
We're always in your hair,
But we're so cute and lovable
You smile when we are there.

(Chorus)

Running through the halls,
Making spirits bright,
Oh what fun it is to sing
A silly song so right.

(Chorus)

• •

4.4 Song line answers

LEVEL	Advanced
TIME	20 minutes
AIM	To use idiomatic phrases in suitable contexts.
PREPARATION	Prepare a list of familiar lines from songs (see examples below) that might be used as answers to start off the interviews. Give a few examples that will fire students' imagination.
	This is an interview with an Austrian political candidate (from a teacher workshop in 1986).

EXAMPLES

1 **Interviewer:** Why are you running for office?
A: 'I am just a poor boy though my story's seldom told, I have squandered all your money ...'

2 **Interviewer:** What would you like from the voters?
A: 'Love me tender, love me true ...'

3 **Interviewer:** What is your programme for the average man?
A: 'Free beer for all the workers, free beer for all the workers!'

4 **Interviewer:** What is your comment on the Austrian budget?
A: 'There's a hole in the bucket, dear Liza, dear Liza ...'

5 **Interviewer:** How would you characterize your relationship with opposition politicians?
A: 'Strangers in the night, exchanging glances ...'

6 **Interviewer:** What are your plans in case you lose the election?
A: 'I'm leaving on a jet plane ...'

Phrases from 1988 songs as answers to interview questions:
– Who's that girl?
– Wish me love a wishing well, kiss and tell
– Born in the USA
– I wanna dance with somebody
– Under the boardwalk
– Boys Boys Boys
– Dirty Diana, no
– What's love got to do, got to do with it?
– Help, I need somebody
– I'm leaving on a jet plane
– You got the look
– Never gonna give you up, never gonna let you down

Phrases from golden oldies:
– Words don't come easy to me
– I'm singing in the rain
– Strangers in the night
– Let it be, let it be
– The answer, my friend, is blowing in the wind
– Like a bridge over troubled water
– Yesterday, all my troubles seemed so far away
– Your cheatin' heart
– You ain't nothin' but a hound dog
– If I had a hammer

IN CLASS

1 Give out the list of possible songs and sample lines.

2 Tell the students briefly how to do the activity (say for example: *The director of the school was asked what he thought of the new students this year and he answered* (sing), *'Yesterday, all my troubles seemed so far away, now it looks as though they're here to stay.'*).

3 Ask students to work in pairs. They look at the song lines, think of someone they would like to interview, and write questions to fit some of the lines.

4 When they have finished writing, they can perform the interview for the class.

VARIATION

With advanced-level classes working on literature, a more sophisticated task can be done. Students record their questions and then find and record portions of different pop songs as answers. A student in a literature class once did a highly successful interview of King Lear in which he answers 'You may be right, I may be crazy' (The Rolling Stones). This variation requires more preparation for the students and more time to carry out.

REMARKS

This activity is relatively easy to do if the students start with the answers (the lines from songs), then try to think of a suitable interviewee and suitable questions. If they start with questions, most students will find it too difficult to find song lines as answers (see Variation above).

4.5 Partial song dictation

LEVEL

Intermediate to advanced

TIME

15 minutes

AIM

To encourage students to create and predict.

PREPARATION

1 Find a song which the class would enjoy but which is not known to them.

2 Prepare hand-outs of the lyrics (see the examples below).

IN CLASS

1 Dictate the first few lines, or partial lines, and ask the students to complete the rest of the verse, either in rhyme or in prose. Tell them that they will be hearing the song later, but that they should write their own words first.

2 When they have finished, let them share what they have written with a partner. Then ask for volunteers to share what they have written with the whole class.

3 Hand out the lyrics and ask the students to compare the themes that they developed to the ones in the actual song.

4 Finally, play the song.

EXAMPLE

I'm the Great Pretender: **Freddy Mercury**
Partial text: Finish line 2 and write two more lines.

Oh, yes. I'm the great pretender
Pretending . . .

One student's version

Oh yes. I'm the great pretender
Pretending I understand
I smile and look interested
But I'm not here.

4.6   Mass distance dictation

LEVEL   **All levels**

TIME   **10–15 minutes**

AIM   To practise giving and receiving dictations, using selective listening and exaggerated pronunciation; to have fun.

PREPARATION Prepare on slips of paper two sections of a song, labelled A and B. Prepare several songs. You will also need some adhesive or sticky tape.

IN CLASS   1 While the class is busy with another activity, stick the slips of paper up on the wall, either in a neighbouring classroom, in the corridor, or on the front wall of the classroom. (The greater the distance, the more the students have to exercise their short-term memory.)

2 Organize the class into pairs and explain that one member of each pair should take a pencil and go and select a song, write their name at the bottom of the paper, and then memorize as much as they can of the first few lines.

3 They then come back and dictate it to their partners, who write it down. The first students can go back to look at the songs several times until they have finished their part (A). To encourage selective listening (since many people will be speaking at the same time) and exaggerated pronunciation, I put the writers on one side of the room and I tell the dictating partners not to get any closer than about three metres to their partners.

4 After the first person has finished the first verse, or after four or five minutes, the partners can change places—the one who was writing then dictates part B, and the other writes.

5 After they have finished, tell the students to bring their songs back into the classroom to compare what they have written.

VARIATION

If you are worried about the amount of disturbance or noise outside, display the songs on the walls of the classroom and tell partners to whisper their dictations to their partners. However, note that this way reduces the time between reading the lines and saying them (and there is less exercise of short-term memory). It also reduces the amount of exaggerated pronunciation, selective listening, and fun! But it does have the advantage that those dictating can see what their partners are writing and correct them on the spot.

4.7   Changing the texts

LEVEL

All levels

TIME

5–20 minutes

AIM

To practise lexical and grammatical categories, and see the semantic changes that result.

PREPARATION

1 Choose a song that has a strong story (for example, *The Boxer, Marvellous Little Toy, Help Me Make It Through The Night*).

2 Prepare hand-outs of the song lyrics. Make enough copies for the whole class.

IN CLASS

1 Give out your hand-out. Ask the students to read the song and do one (or more) of the following:
a. Change all the verbs from present to past (or some other verb tense).
b. Change the pronouns from first to second or third person, and make other appropriate changes.
c. Change adjectives and verbs to give the opposite meaning.
d. Change gender references from male to female (or vice versa). See the example below.

2 Let the students work in pairs and then discuss the different versions:
Is the meaning significantly changed? Why is one better than another? etc.

EXAMPLE

Leaving on a Jet Plane

All my bags are packed, I'm ready to go
I'm standing here outside your door
I hate to wake you up to say
goodbye

Re-written, this would read:

1 All my bags **were** packed, I **was**
ready to go ...   *or*

2 All **your** bags are packed, **you're**
ready to go ...   *or*

3 All my bags are **un**packed, I'm **not**
ready to go ...

REMARKS

1 This activity is a good lead-in to more elaborate songwriting later.

2 Make sure you actually try out the exercise beforehand to ensure that it works with the song you have chosen.

4.8   Group songwriting

LEVEL

All levels

TIME

5–15 minutes

AIM

To share a composition task, and to learn to use language creatively.

PREPARATION

For the Variation, prepare a list of at least six stem sentences for the students to finish (for example, *The sun is like . . . ,
Love is like . . .*).

IN CLASS

1 Ask the students to form groups of five or six. Each student in turn writes down on a piece of paper one word, a partial thought, a complete phrase, or any combination of the above, and passes the paper on to the next person in the group.

2 If the students are doing the one-word version, ask them to write down their favourite word then pass the paper on to the next person. They go round the group three times. Tell them that they are writing a kind of poetry and that it does not need to make sense right away as they will edit it later! On the fourth round, each student writes a short sentence with at least two of the words they have written themselves. On the fifth round, they have to write another sentence with one word that was not used and one that was. On the sixth round they have to write a sentence with all three of their own words. On the seventh round, the students must edit their own paper in order to make it into a song-poem, and add the words *I*, *you*, and *love*, unless they are already included. They can change their text as they wish—they are the editors!

3 If the students want to share their compositions with the rest of the class, encourage them to do so.

4 They may also want to put them to music.

VARIATION

A variation consists of everybody writing down one thing on a given theme and then giving it to one student to put together cohesively.

1 Ask the whole class, in groups of five or six, to complete the sentence *The sun is like.* . .

2 When they have finished, they pass their slips of paper to one member of the group. You then ask them to complete another stem sentence (*Love is like . . .*). They then pass these to another member of the group. By the time they have completed six such sentences, each member of the each group will have five or six slips of paper with sentences on the same topic.

3 Each student then arranges the sentences in some sort of poetic order and edits them as a song-poem.

Note: Your class will use a lot of rough paper for this activity. Encourage them to save it for recycling!

REMARKS

1 Songwriting can arise from an activity such as 2.4 (*My favourite moment*), a guided visualization in which the students write, using the vocabulary of their five senses. It is important to teach your students the discipline of 'chopping', that is, editing unnecessary words and giving the essence of their inspiration in clear images and impressions. Show them a song like *Country Roads* as an example of partial sentences.

2 Those who want to try to put any of the lyrics to music should be encouraged to do so. It is not as difficult as it seems. The musician will need to exercise artistic licence to rearrange the lyrics if need be.

3 Some students may be apprehensive about writing poetry, and may find it easier if we call it songwriting. Conversely, some teachers who regularly encourage their students to write poetry may think themselves unqualified to teach songwriting. In fact, because songs are often (though not always) linguistically simpler than most poetry, they can serve as a gentle lead-in to it.

4.9   Poetic analysis of lyrics

LEVEL

Intermediate to advanced

TIME

Variable (and for homework)

AIM

To teach a few poetic elements in pop songs; to stimulate the real use of the foreign language to express personal meanings.

PREPARATION	1 Make a list of the structural and poetic items you wish students to identify. For example: title, stanza (or verse), refrain (or chorus), bridge, verse-chorus structure, hook, rhyme, rhyme scheme, alliteration, personification, etc.
	2 Find a song with a typical rhyming scheme and structure. Analyse it yourself first to see which elements are there and which are not.
	3 Make copies for the class and collect some other song texts for the students to analyse.
IN CLASS	1 Pass out your example. Ask students to identify your list of items. Then, go over the list with the whole class to make sure everyone has understood.
	2 You may need to pay special attention to verse-chorus structure. For example, we might label verse as A, chorus as B, and a bridge as C. So a song like *Blowing in the Wind* which simply goes verse-chorus over and over is ABABAB, while *Country Roads* has a bridge instead of a third verse ABABCB. And *Yesterday* has an AACA structure.
	You may also want to pay special attention to the rhyming scheme. Verses in *Blowing in the Wind* is simply AAA, BBB, CCC, while that of *Country Roads* are AABB.
	3 Give a different song to each person in a pair and ask them to identify the poetic elements and structures. If they already have a corpus of songs that have been used, ask them to select a song in the corpus to analyse.
	4 Then have the students explain their analysis to their partner.
VARIATION	Of course, compositions or class presentations can be done following this, either on a single song or on the contrast between songs. A top ten can also be done to judge the best lyrics based on poetic analysis.
REMARKS	For really advanced classes, simply consult the many poetry analysis texts for further terms and points to analyse. However, be careful not to turn a conversation class that enjoys treating songs conversationally into a literature lecture class. (See also Gray 1991 on this.)

4.10   Lyric-writing contest

LEVEL	**All levels**
TIME	**Variable** (or to be given as homework)
AIM	To stimulate the use of language to express personal meanings.
PREPARATION	1 Prepare a hand-out (see Sample Hand-out below).
	2 Make enough copies for the whole class.

**SAMPLE
HAND-OUT**

Pop song lyric contest

Deadline for submissions is ...
(To be judged by your
classmates.)
Songwriting observations
1 The lines you write do not
   have to rhyme.
2 You do not need to use full
   sentences (look at *Country
   Roads*, for an example).
3 Your song does not have to
   be very long. Most pop songs
are about 250 words long, but
use only about 75 different
words because lines are
repeated a lot, especially the
chorus.
4 Submissions should be on one
   page (in two copies), with your
   name on the back of one copy.
   (The judges will be given a
   copy without the author's
   name.)
5 Hand it in to ... before the
   deadline.

IN CLASS

1 Explain to the students that you are going to display the words of seven or eight songs around the room.

2 Ask the students to read and rate them from A–G/H ('A' being the one they like the most, etc.).

3 When the students have completed their choices, tabulate the results (A = 2, B = 1) and then let them discuss in small groups why some of the lyrics got high scores and others did not.

4 Finally, ask the students to write their own song lyrics by a certain date. At this point, give them the hand-out you have prepared.

5 After the deadline, the students' lyrics are displayed around the room and students put an (A) against their first choice and (B) for their second. A top ten is then calculated (for example, A = 2, B = 1) and announced.

VARIATION

This activity can be carried out in one class or, on a larger scale, in a school or in the community. The judges in a wider context could be a mixture of musicians, teachers, students, and disc-jockeys.
It might even be appropriate to produce a booklet of some or all of the lyrics.

REMARKS

Activities 4.4, 4.6, and 4.12 are all good lead-ins to this activity. All these activities already begin to focus on rewriting song lyrics. Activity 4.9 also considerable improves the quality of students' compositions.

4.11   The 'English' of pop lyrics

LEVEL   Advanced

TIME   Variable

AIM   To make students aware of different registers of English.

PREPARATION   1 Find a few songs that contain different registers of English (poetic, colloquial, archaic, slang, and non-standard usage).

2 Prepare a hand-out such as the one below.

3 Make enough copies for the whole class.

4 Collect song lyrics that the students have previously expressed an interest in.

IN CLASS   1 Give the students the hand-out you have prepared and go over it for comprehension.

2 Then give them some of the song lyrics that they have expressed interest in and ask them to look through them for similar examples.

**SAMPLE
HAND-OUT**

THE LANGUAGE OF POP

Some people think that pop songs are like poetry. Some say they are written in modern colloquial English. Others say that they contain unintelligible slang, with non-standard grammar mixed with archaic expressions. In reality, the language of pop can be all of these things.

Examples of different features of pop lyrics:

Poetic

Hello darkness, my old friend. (Paul Simon) (personification)

And every move you make
Every bond you break
Every step you take
I'll be watching you. (Sting) (alliteration, parallel structures, rhyme)

For long you live and high you fly,
And smiles you'll give and tears you'll cry. (Pink Floyd) (inversion)

Colloquial

Take it easy. (Eagles)

It is anybody's ballgame
It is everybody's fight. (John Prine)

Archaic

There's an iron train a-travellin'
That's been a-rollin' through the years. (Bob Dylan)

Now since my baby left me
I've found a new place to dwell. (Elvis Presley)

Slang and non-standard English

I'm bad. (Michael Jackson)

Feelin' Groovy. (Paul Simon)

Ain't got no distractions
Can't hear no buzzers and bells. (Pete Townsend) (subjectless, *ain't*, double negatives)

You ain't nothin' but a hound dog. (Elvis Presley) (*ain't*, double negative)

Sun is shining, the weather is sweet
Make you want to move your dancing feet ...
When the morning gather the rainbow
Want you to know, I'm a rainbow too. (Bob Marley) (missing articles and subjects)

VARIATION	Instead of collecting and giving the song lyrics to the students yourself, ask them (for homework) to look at a song that they like and to try to find as many different features as possible in it.
REMARKS	A song rich in poetical and structural features is Billy Joel's *She's Always a Woman*.

Acknowledgement
I was first tuned in to this activity by Dennis Davy (1985).

4.12   Discourse analysis of pop songs

LEVEL	**Very advanced**
TIME	**Part of two or three classes**
PREPARATION	Make copies of the hand-out below and collect some songs for students to analyse.
SAMPLE HAND-OUT	

The who, where, and when of pop song lyrics

In a recent analysis of 50 pop songs, it was found that all songs but one had an *I* referent, while 88 per cent had a *you*, with only one each of these referents being specified by proper names. Of course, the major theme is *love* in one of its various relationship stages – beginning, ongoing, or breaking up. It seems that the stereotypical message of most songs is *I love you*, but we are never told who *I* and *you* are.

In addition, only six of the 50 song lyrics explicitly mention the sex of the singer (male or female) and only 17 mention the sex of *you*. This means that usually the pronouns could refer to either sex for either sex. Furthermore, a pop singer's voice is often not distinctively male or female. Thus, we have a type of omniphonic voice, which could be of either sex, speaking to us about undesignated *you*s and *I*s.

Another point of interest is that 94 per cent of the songs mention no time reference and 80 per cent have no place reference. These characteristics allow songs to 'happen' whenever and wherever they are heard. Listeners can integrate them into their own world and the people in the songs can become people in their own mind. The 'ghost discourse' which constitutes a song lyric only takes on meaning and form in the minds and environments of the people who use the songs. Thus, we can only say what a song 'means' by focusing on listeners and their interpretations, not by looking at the song itself.

Lastly, the imprecise and highly affective elements of pop songs allow us to use them as 'teddy-bears-in-the-ear': they are verbal 'strokes' which can be ignored or deliberately misunderstood at no risk; like a teddy bear, the song is still 'there' for us. The widespread use of the Walkman makes this analogy even more concrete.

For discussion

Do you agree with the above analysis of pop songs? To what extent do you think the majority of songs fit the above description?

Assignment

Find a recent pop song that you like and analyse it in the light of the above description, answering the following questions:

1 Are the pronouns explictly designated?
2 Are the place and time mentioned?
3 Is the sex of the singer implied or stated in the lyrics?

4 Could someone who did not know the singer tell whether they are male or female?
5 How do you, personally, understand the song? What do you think of when you hear it? How does it make you feel?
6 If there is a film or video clip of the song, do you mentally identify with that when you hear the song, or do you have other mental images?
7 To what extent does your song fit the description in the passage above? Is it stereotypical or is it an exception?

IN CLASS

1 Give out the prepared hand-outs.

2 Set the assignment.

3 Ask the students to bring to class a song they have analysed.

4 In groups of four, they present what they have found to each other and compare their findings.

5 Then each student can write a short report of their analysis, including a statement of the degree to which the song fits the description in the hand-out, how their song compared with those of others in their group, and the extent to which they think the analysis in the hand-out is an accurate generalization.

4.13   Photo-story dialogue writing

LEVEL   Intermediate to advanced

TIME   Part of two or three classes

AIM   To help students contextualize the language in songs.

PREPARATION

1 Select a few narrative songs, or songs for which a narrative can be easily imagined, and that the students have expressed interest in (for example, *Leaving on a Jet Plane* (John Denver), *She's Leaving Home* (The Beatles), *Father and Son* (Cat Stevens), etc.).

2 Also collect a few photo-stories to show as examples to the class.

IN CLASS

1 Show the students some examples of photo-stories and explain that you would like them to do something similar, based on a song. They do not have to stick strictly to the song, but can create a more complete context surrounding the song.

2 Ask the students in groups of four or five to choose different songs and plan the various scenes they want to photograph (for example, a boy standing outside an apartment door, the sun rising behind a taxi, etc.).

3 They then write out the dialogue to go with each picture and any subscript (that is, explanation at the bottom of the pictures, for example: *It's early morn and the dawn is breaking. The impatient taxi driver honks his horn.*).

4 Point out that once they have taken the photographs, the dialogue and subscript may need rewriting.

5 The photographic session can be done either in the class/school environment or after school for homework. The students should use black and white film. Encourage the students to develop the pictures themselves if they know how and if there is a photographic studio available.

6 Finally, the students paste the pictures in sequences onto sheets of paper, write the speech bubbles (encircled with black ink), and stick them onto the photographs, together with the narrative subscript.

7 When they have their photo-story complete, ask them to write a page of acknowledgements to the writers of the script, the photographers, and layout team.

8 Display the photo-story in the classroom.

VARIATION 1

The photo-story could be made part of a larger class newsletter (see activity 1.7).

VARIATION 2

Students take a series of photos of the school staff and add lines from pop songs in their speech bubbles.

VARIATION 3

If you have a video camera, the students could take different shots of everyday events and surroundings, but put them to humorously selected music.

Acknowledgement
I first read about this in an article by Kathleen Knott in *Practical English Teacher*.

4.14   Songs and story writing

LEVEL

Intermediate to advanced

TIME

30–50 minutes

AIM

To expose students to the conventions used in different song types and styles, and to provide the input to be used in story construction.

PREPARATION

1 Find a few songs with stereotypical language and images for the genre (for example with country music: *cowboy, drinking, pick-up truck, prison, cheating on lovers*, etc; with Bubblegum Pop: *dream-sweet love, forever*, etc.).

2 Prepare a gap-fill exercise on the basis of one of the songs.

3 Make enough copies for the whole class.

IN CLASS

1 Do the gap-fill exercise or a video-viewing of the song first to familiarize the students with it.

2 Then ask them if they think it is a typical song of its kind, and if so, what makes it typical.

3 Ask the students to list all the cliché phrases and images for the genre.

4 Then ask the students in pairs to write another verse to the song, a letter, or a short story using these cliché images. Tell them to exaggerate the 'corniness' in order to make it funny.

5 When they have finished, ask the students to form groups of four and to read each other's work, correct each other, and explain and discuss if necessary.

VARIATION 1

(This variation requires the co-operation of members of staff of the school/institute.) The students first write typical (cliché) letters and then their own real letters (which they sign with a pseudonym) to staff at the school. The teachers who have agreed to take part in this activity write back cliché letters to their secret admirers. This can be fun for students and teachers alike.

VARIATION 2

1 Choose a typical country song and get students to think about the conventions in literary genres (the Western, spy thriller, etc.)

2 They then write stories using these conventions. This variation is easier for the students if they have first had some practice in identifying the conventions in songs.

3 Students should be aware that a song is just a 'snapshot' and that in writing we have to contextualize, and fill in what happened before and after the moment-in-time of the song. (See Brown and Helgesen 1989.)

REMARKS	Rod Nash, in personal correspondance with me, has stressed the importance of sensitizing students to the different conventions of a variety of song types, so that they can better grasp the conventionality of their own chosen music.

4.15   Songs to literature

LEVEL	Upper-intermediate to advanced
TIME	Variable
AIM	To underline the parallelism between music and other artistic expression.
PREPARATION	Look for songs with themes analogous to those of a literary work you are currently studying with your class.
EXAMPLES	**Similarity of themes between books/films and songs**

For the book/film *Ordinary People* (by Judith Guest), the following themes could be highlighted by certain songs: Sincerity versus superficiality:
True Colors (Cindy Lauper)
Love for a father:
Leader of the Band (Dan Fogelberg)

For *The Great Gatsby* (by Fitzgerald) and materialism: Madonna's *Material Girl* and Marilyn Monroe's *Diamonds are a Girl's Best Friend*. Don McLean's *American Pie* treats the American Dream.

For *The Old Man and the Sea* (Hemingway): Ralph McTell's *The Streets of London* and Jimmy Buffet's *He went to Paris* introduce the old age theme and Buffet's *Mother Mother Ocean* treats rapport with the sea.

IN CLASS	1 Either play a song as an introduction to the theme before starting a literary work, or use a song to illustrate and reinforce what has already been talked about in a work. Drawing parallels between the themes in older novels and the themes in current songs makes the novels more relevant for many students. However, there are always slight variations in the ways the themes are treated and in the intensity of their treatment in each work.

2 Stimulate discussion by asking how they are different, and which one the students prefer and why.

4.16   Song feedback

LEVEL	All levels
TIME	10–20 minutes
AIM	To teach vocabulary and to develop critical awareness.

PREPARATION

1 Some time before you do this activity, ask your students how they would describe a song they like/do not like. Ask them to list as many terms as possible on a piece of paper. Collect the papers and use the students' words and phrases to construct a feedback form.

2 Either prepare the feedback form yourself or, in a previous class, ask your students to prepare one (see Sample Feedback Form below).

3 Make copies of the form for the whole class.

4 Choose a song to play in class.

SAMPLE FEEDBACK FORM

How would you describe this song?

1 = not at all; 6 = very much.

Circle the number of your choice.

warm	1 2 3 4 5 6
gentle	1 2 3 4 5 6
lively	1 2 3 4 5 6
soft	1 2 3 4 5 6
boring	1 2 3 4 5 6
yellow	1 2 3 4 5 6
simple	1 2 3 4 5 6
fun	1 2 3 4 5 6
repetitive	1 2 3 4 5 6
good beat	1 2 3 4 5 6
good instrumentation	1 2 3 4 5 6
good lyrics	1 2 3 4 5 6
socio-politically engaged	1 2 3 4 5 6
disorganized	1 2 3 4 5 6
too long	1 2 3 4 5 6

makes me want to dance	1 2 3 4 5 6
inspiring	1 2 3 4 5 6
soothing	1 2 3 4 5 6
I want to hear it again	1 2 3 4 5 6
I would give it to a friend	1 2 3 4 5 6

I think the person singing is:

sincere	1 2 3 4 5 6
in love	1 2 3 4 5 6
excited	1 2 3 4 5 6
angry	1 2 3 4 5 6
bored	1 2 3 4 5 6
boring	1 2 3 4 5 6

I would like to meet the singer

1 2 3 4 5 6

Can you imagine saying the words to someone? 1 2 3 4 5 6

Write your evaluation of the song in full sentences on the back of this form.

IN CLASS

1 Hand out the feedback form before listening to the song. Go over the vocabulary and elicit questions.

2 Then play the song and ask the students to fill in their forms as they listen.

3 When they have finished, give them five to ten minutes to write out their feedback as continuous prose at the bottom of the form (advanced students).

4 Working in pairs, each student compares reactions with a partner.

VARIATION 1

1 Tell the students not to write their names on their papers, but to mark it with a secret code or name, so that they can find their own paper later.

2 Collect the papers and redistribute them at random.

3 The students read the papers they have been given and on the back write a paragraph about the 'mystery' person's evaluation of the song and what they think the person is like.

4 When all have finished writing, they go round the classroom asking questions, and trying to find out whose paper they have. When they have found the 'author' they show what they wrote (and have a good laugh!).

VARIATION 2

The feedback form can be used to introduce or reinforce grammatical structures (conditionals, question forms with *do*, comparatives and superlatives, etc.).

REMARKS

1 There is no 'best form' and we are not doing scientific research. The 'best' criteria (and vocabulary) to use are those of your students.

2 Creating a feedback form is a learning experience for everyone.

3 Students may be prepared to discuss at length whether a term is positive or negative.

4.17 Cultural comparison and contrasts of music

LEVEL

Intermediate to advanced

TIME

60 minutes ($\times 2$)

AIM

To practise comparison and contrast in writing.

PREPARATION

(This activity is designed for classes of mixed cultures.)
1 Collect together a selection of about four different kinds of songs from different countries.

2 Prepare a chart similar to the one below.

3 Make enough copies for the whole class.

SAMPLE CHART

Musical selections		1	2	3	4
Type of music:	vocal/instrumental				
Instruments:	one/a few/many				
Tempo:	fast/slow				
Mood:	happy/sad/other				
Purpose:	dancing/listening/other				

IN CLASS

Lesson one

1 Distribute the chart if you have made one, or write it up on the board.

2 Tell the students that over several sessions they are going to hear very different kinds of music from many different cultures.

3 Help the students to identify the kind of vocabulary they will need to compare and contrast the different pieces.

4 Write this vocabulary on the board and 'flesh out' the chart.

5 Play the four short pieces.

6 Students note their own responses.

Lesson two

1 For the following session, ask students to bring in a piece of typical music from their countries or a piece that they like. These may be contemporary or traditional.

2 Play each piece.

3 The students describe the pieces within the terms of the chart, discussing each one as they go along.

4 Once all the selections have been played and compared orally, the students write short compositions comparing the different pieces of music they have heard.

VARIATION

Give the chart to the students to use for journal writing for a few minutes every day (see activity 3.9). Conduct a short discussion session before the writing to elicit new vocabulary. In monolingual classes, you may decide to ask just a few students to bring in selections of different kinds of music.

REMARKS

While this activity encourages vocabulary expansion and oral practice, the ultimate aim is for the students to produce a well drafted composition comparing and contrasting different types of songs. Good composition work requires preliminary discussion. A rough 'oral draft' will make the subsequent writing easier and better.

Acknowledgement

This activity is an interpretation of an idea by J. van Cleve (1984).

4.18 Unknown songs and artists

LEVEL

Intermediate to advanced

TIME

30–60 minutes

AIM

To practise the language of prediction.

PREPARATION

1 Choose recordings of songs by four singers of the same sex whom you are sure your students are not familiar with.

2 Find large pictures of each of them.

IN CLASS

1 Put the pictures on the wall or board so all can see them. Number them 1, 2, 3, and 4.

2 Tell the students you will play four songs (A, B, C, and D), one by each of the artists in the pictures. They must decide which song goes with which picture.

3 Ask the students to form groups of four and to write down their guesses and their reasons (for example, *I think singer 1 sings song C, because she looks like a rocker and this one is in a rock n' roll style. The others look too gentle to sing song C.*).

4 After writing down their guesses they compare them in their groups.

5 Finally, draw the following grid on the board and ask for the votes for each one by a show of hands.

	A	B	C	D
1	2	6	12	0
2				
3				
4				

6 After you have counted all the votes and noted them on the board, circle the correct box.

VARIATION 1	You can select songs in the target language or in one or more unknown languages. Students then can discuss what they think the singer is singing about on the basis of the vocal characteristics. This practises the language of prediction (*It must be a . . . It could be about . . .*).
VARIATION 2	You can make this activity reading-focused by asking the students to match photographs and articles about artists.
VARIATION 3	1 Another interesting variation is to hand out three different lyrics and play an instrumental version of one of them. (See Calvert 1980.) 2 Students then have to see which lyrics fit the music and discuss the parallel structures of phrasing and rhythm in both music and language.
REMARKS	1 A useful lead-in to this activity is 3.1. 2 It is best not to choose recent pop songs for this activity, but country, or some other genre probably less familiar to your students.

4.19   Singing, singing, singing

LEVEL	**All levels**
TIME	**5–10 minutes**
AIM	To sing, practise pronunciation and intonation, and have fun.
PREPARATION	1 Choose a song that the students have shown interest in. 2 Write out the lyrics and make copies for the whole class.
IN CLASS	I have not talked much about singing so far, but it is an obvious thing to do and one that many students will enjoy the most. 1 Hand out the song sheets you have prepared. 2 Play the song you have chosen. 3 Encourage the students to sing along with you or the tape. Stop the tape at intervals for the students to learn and repeat the tune. 4 After the students have learnt a song, there are many ways of performing it which are fun and reinforce learning.
VARIATION 1	Divide the class (down the middle, according to gender, etc.) and give different parts of the song to each group. Alternatively, at the end of a song, ask first the boys to sing the chorus and then the girls.

VARIATION 2	Mix up songs, singing a verse from one and a chorus from another, or make a medley of hits.

VARIATION 3	Start a choir, song club, or folksong club.

REMARKS

1 It is helpful if you can play an instrument, preferably a guitar, as an accompaniment leaves the students less exposed. Or you could play the tape of the song to give the students something to follow. Play it loud at first, then lower the volume and let the students' voices take over.

2 Singing activities seem easiest with young children (see Section 6) and teenagers (before self-consciousness sets in), but many groups will surprise you and turn out to love singing.

4.20   Song rotation dictation

LEVEL

Intermediate to advanced

TIME

50 minutes

AIM

To practise listening comprehension, dictation, and to have fun. The songs collected from your students for this activity can be used in later classes. This and the following activities in this section are designed for use in a language laboratory.

PREPARATION

1 You need to have as many cassettes as you have students. Each cassette should have a different song recorded on it. You could prepare these yourself (if you like being overworked!). However, to reduce your workload and increase your students' motivation, ask them to bring you a song that they are interested in working with, which they have recorded at the beginning of a cassette. They should also tell you what song they are going to bring, so that they do not all bring the same one. Set a date by which all cassettes must be ready. Remind the students to put their names on the cassette.

2 You may also want to stipulate that the singers' words should be intelligible, because you will be using them for a dictation exercise.

IN CLASS

1 Give each student a cassette (other than your own) and a sheet of paper. Tell them they have only five minutes to listen to their song and to transcribe as much of it as possible. Signal the students after five minutes (I blink the lights on and off). They then pass their paper and cassette to the next booth (you will have to transfer a cassette up to the front booth each time).

2 After the first cassettes are passed on, and from then on, they have to rewind the cassettes to the beginning, listen, and read what the previous listener wrote, check to see if they agree with the transcription, correct it if they think there are mistakes, and then try to carry it further.

If the song has been fully transcribed after the first 30 minutes, students still listen to it and check what the others have written, correcting what they can or putting in alternatives if they are not sure. If cassettes are changed every five minutes, each student will have worked on ten songs in a 50-minute class, done a lot of listening comprehension, and practised dictation and student/student corrections.

VARIATION 1

You may want to use just a few different songs with several copies for lower-level classes. That way if the students do not understand much the first time, they will hear it again later and have the help of someone else's further transcriptions.

VARIATION 2

Another aid may be to write out the first line yourself.

VARIATION 3

At the end of class you can ask the students which song they liked the most and make a top ten list.

VARIATION 4

For homework, the student who initially brought the cassette can take the paper and cassette home and write out a clean copy of the words. They should hand in both the clean version and the dictation to you with the cassette. In this way the students do a lot of manipulation with material that they like and you get a stock of material to exploit in later classes.

4.21   Recording opinions

LEVEL

Intermediate to advanced

TIME

50 minutes

AIM

To stimulate language production and opinions; to encourage listening by other students.

PREPARATION

You need to do activity 4.19 above, or assemble enough texts and cassettes for the whole class.

IN CLASS

1 Give a cassette and lyric sheet to each student. Ask them to listen to the song on the tape and immediately afterwards to record a comment about the song. This can be information or a reaction to the song, for example, *This is Madonna singing a song from her latest album* or *I like the beat*.

2 After they have done this, they pass the cassette and lyric sheet to the next booth.

3 They then listen to the new song and the comments of the previous listener before recording their own comment.
The rules are that no one is allowed to repeat what a previous person has said, and each person must speak clearly!

4 After everyone has heard five or six songs, they stop. The last person transcribes all the comments at the bottom, or on the back of the lyric sheet. The tape is then put in the language lab library for others to listen to when they wish.

VARIATION

This could also be done as a tape exchange outside of the lab class. (See activity 4.24.)

4.22   Open selection song lab

LEVEL

Intermediate to advanced

TIME

10–20 minutes

AIM

To encourage independent learning for a portion of the lab class.

PREPARATION

Prepare enough copies of the form in the example and assemble a wide choice of cassettes.

EXAMPLE

```
Song reaction          by............... Date
Title
Artist
Style
Length
Introduction
Instrumentation
Vocals
Lyrics
Story-line or situation
Main point
Listener's score for the song:
(1= least good, 6= best)
Prose summary
```

IN CLASS	1 Hand out the forms.

2 At the beginning or end of a lab class, students choose a song to listen to. They fill in the song analysis form as they listen and write a prose summary of their reaction afterwards, using the information from the form.

VARIATION

Past evaluations of the songs by other students can be kept in a folder, or stapled together, and shown to the students after they have done the exercise.

REMARKS

The idea behind the open selection song lab is to allow students to work individually on a stock of songs and lyric sheets. Activities 4.20 and 4.21 help to create this stock.

4.23   Name those songs

LEVEL

All levels

TIME

20–30 minutes

AIM

To have fun and spark their memories concerning song.

PREPARATION

1 At the end of a term or year, mix a tape containing just a few lines of each song you have used with your students. Try not to make them too obvious.

2 Prepare a hand-out with more song titles than the number of songs that you are going to play. (For a more advanced class, only write part of the title, or a few letters, if it is a one-word title.)

3 Also, prepare a separate sheet with a few obscure lines from the same songs on it, but not in the same order as on the cassette. Letter these lines (A) to however many you have.

IN CLASS

1 Hand out the song titles list and explain to your students that they will hear parts of some songs and that they are to write number 1 by the first one they hear, and so forth.

2 Play the tape through twice (or ask the students to make their own copies in their lab booth as they go along, and work through at their speed).

3 Then hand out the obscure lines from the song. Students match up song titles and lines.

4 Finally, ask them to compare their lists with their neighbours. Ask someone to write their list on the board and correct and replay if necessary.

VARIATION

You can increase the complexity by having mistakes in the song titles.

4.24   Tape exchange

LEVEL   **False beginners to advanced**

TIME   **20 minutes** (homework)

AIM   To encourage learner independence and interaction outside the classroom.

PREPARATION   Prepare a hand-out describing how the activity works and what students are to do (see Sample Hand-out).

**SAMPLE
HAND-OUT**

Music tape exchange

1 At home, record one of your favourite songs at the beginning of a 90-minute cassette.
2 Write your English/secret names and the names of the song and the artist(s) on the cassette.
3 After you have recorded the song, record yourself introducing yourself (with your English/secret name, not your real one). Record yourself talking about the song for as long as you like. (You may want to prepare notes, but avoid reading them. Try to speak freely.) You might like to talk about some of the following:
•why you chose that song
•what you like about the music and/or the lyrics
•what you know about the group
•what the song makes you think of
•when you usually play this song.
4 Please bring your recorded cassettes to class on ... .

5 When you hand me your cassettes, I will give them to students in one of my other classes. The students do not know you.
6 The other students will listen to your song. They will then introduce themselves and comment on the song. They will then record a song they like and comment on it for you. They will also write their English/secret name on the cassette, with the title of their song.
7 They will return the cassettes to me and I will give them back to you. After that, it is up to you to continue if you wish. At the end of the year, we will have a party and you will be able to meet your cassette-partner face to face.
Note: There are three rules you must keep:
1 No reading of comments
2 No recording in your own language
3 No time limit.

Note: You may make photocopies of this for classroom use (but please note that copyright law does not normally permit multiple copying of published material).

IN CLASS   1 Go over the hand-out with your students and clear up any questions they may have. You can give the other class the same hand-out, so that they understand what is going on.

2 A few days before the cassettes are due in, remind the students.

REMARKS   Although this activity can be done within one class, it seems to
work better if the students exchange cassettes between classes, so
that the students do not know who the other person is. It is also
more natural to communicate through the cassette. It is not natural
when they know and see the other person every day. It is also fun
for the students to meet their partner at the end of the year.

Acknowledgement
Ken Hartmann first introduced me to a version of this idea. He has
students exchanging cassettes from different schools and he acts
merely as a kind of postman. He even has students from high school
exchanging with students from college. In some cases he says they
go into multiple volumes and continue after leaving his classes.

5 Video song clips

Some pop song videos are like *haikus*, like fantastic short stories put to film and music. Others are simply by-products of a very fast-moving industry from which extremes of quality are to be expected. Video clips, as a relatively new art form, have caught on amazingly fast, principally because they are powerful marketing tools for selling recordings. Few stars release recordings for the youth market today without the backing of videos, and many major films count on important soundtrack sales for publicity and added revenue (for example, *Saturday Night Fever, Dirty Dancing, La Bamba*, etc.)

Videos are also fast becoming mainstream products in themselves, since many collectors prefer them to sound-only recordings. Discothèques are becoming media-equipped to show videos to their clientele. This means that the dancers get the feeling that they can 'dance with the stars'. The experience of 'assimilating' a song as their own becomes even more powerful as large video screens merge with the disco dance floor and the division between broadcast media and the actual physical environment becomes blurred. To a certain extent, the media take over and *become* the physical environment.

As with any new technology, there are usually advantages and disadvantages. My principal pleasures in using videos in the classroom are learning from my students how they evaluate videos, learning with them how to sort out the good from the bad, trying to see if there is something behind the 'flash and thunder', and recognizing that some videos are there just for fun, while others are shockingly meaningful. Others, of course, may have little or no value for us. Learning how to understand the media, to use TV and videos wisely, and not simply to be hypnotized by them, has become a major goal for me and has at times turned using videos into a subject for class discussion. *Video* by Richard Cooper, Mike Lavery, and Mario Rinvolucri, in this series, contains many useful tips.

Music videos can be used successfully with any age group or level of students when the activities are adjusted to them. They can be used at the end of class for a ten minute uplift, or they can be an integral part of one or more lessons. Teachers can start from a text, a sound recording, or an image (or images) and gradually add on the other dimensions.

Sources

I strongly recommend to teachers not to do all the work of gathering song texts, or recording videos, etc. My belief is that they should share this responsibility with the students, and let them choose videos and songs, let them present them in class, and prepare exercises for their classmates. This will give them more active control over and responsibility for their own learning. Videos should not be used for 'baby-sitting' purposes. Students may be content to be passive watchers, but we, as teachers, need to encourage student interaction with the video, and involve the students initially in predicting, describing, commenting, and sharing their perceptions. (I am indebted to Cynthia Beresford for originally showing me how this can be done.)

Getting started

1 Ask the students themselves what kind of videos they like and what they could bring to present in class. Feedback from the class could be tabulated and displayed in the classroom.

2 Distribute a questionnaire (to find out the amount of viewing time and types of videos students like, and whether they prefer listening or viewing, whether they collect clips, and so on). If they are interested, the students can develop their own questionnaire to do in class, in the school, or outside, in the community. They can then draw up a top ten video list and write a report or newsletter (see activities 1.1, 1.2, and 1.3).

3 Discuss with your students what impact a song has on its own as opposed to being heard and seen on video. Are there any songs that they liked before, but not after seeing the video? Are there any songs they liked only after seeing the video?

5.1   Brainstorming

LEVEL	**Intermediate to advanced** (teenagers and adults)
TIME	**10–15 minutes**
AIM	To encourage students' independence and responsibility for their own learning; to promote fluency.
PREPARATION	None.
IN CLASS	**1** Tell your students that you are considering using video clips in class, and ask them if they can suggest some ways in which they could be used to learn English. Let them think about it individually for a minute or two and then discuss in pairs or small groups. Ask them to write down their ideas. **2** Next, ask the students to list their current favourite videos and any old ones that they especially like.

3 Ask the students if they would be willing to lend you their favourite video cassette to show in class, and perhaps also to supply you with information and articles on the groups, song texts, and pictures involved.

REMARKS

Many of the activities in this and other sections originated from suggestions made by students in sessions such as this one. Your students will be delighted if you pick their brains for a change!

5.2 Freeze-frame

LEVEL

All levels

TIME

5 minutes

AIM

To practise guessing, prediction, and descriptions, using the simple present, present continuous, and conditionals.

PREPARATION

Most video machines have a freeze-frame button which you can use to stop the tape on one frame.

1 Find two frames of a singer to freeze in the early part of the video.

2 Prepare a list of questions that you might ask about the first frame, for example:
– *What can you see?*
– *What are the colours?*
– *What is he/she wearing?*
– *Where is this person? Can you guess?*
– *What is in the background?*
– *What expression is on the person's face?*
– *Is the person moving, standing, sitting?*
– *What kind of personality do you think this person has?*
– *Would you sit next to him/her on a bus?*
– *What do you think they are singing about?*
– *What do you think they might do in the video?*

IN CLASS

1 Switch on the video recorder and freeze the first frame.

2 Demonstrate the activity by asking the questions you have prepared.

3 Next, turn the video recorder round, or arrange the seats so that only half the students can see the screen.

4 Tell one half of the students to describe what they see to a partner in the other half. The students who cannot see the screen can ask questions of those who can. (It does not matter if they overhear each other and repeat the same things—pseudo-cheating is one of the more powerful ways of learning!)

VARIATION 1 Dim the brightness control or make it too bright, so that the image is very difficult to see. Ask students to guess what might be happening. Gradually adjust the picture and let the students continue to guess what they see.

VARIATION 2 Turn your back to the video, or stand behind it, and tell the class you cannot see the screen. Ask them to describe the picture to you. Ask questions if necessary concerning the number of people, objects, the background, colours, etc.

REMARKS 1 A freeze-frame is like a moment in time. Like a photograph, part of its power is that it prompts us to imagine what went before and what comes after. With video, we actually get to see that.

2 Any prediction exercises can, with a freeze-frame, be verified at a later stage.

5.3 Prediction vocabulary list

LEVEL **Beginners to advanced**

TIME **5–10 minutes**

AIM To get students to use cues to build possible contexts; to familiarize them with vocabulary before viewing; to practise simple present and past tenses of action verbs.

PREPARATION 1 Prepare a list of action verbs that come up in the video (see the example below).

2 Make enough copies for the whole class.

IN CLASS 1 Distribute hand-outs of the list, and explain that these words will help the students to describe what they are going to see in the video. Let them work in pairs to go through the list. If they do not know a word, they can also ask their partner or another group for help.

EXAMPLE

A list of action verbs for *Like a Prayer* by Madonna

run	fall	get up	walk	enter	cry
hold	sing	kneel	kiss	open	smile
drop	whisper	leave	lie (down)	clap	dance
sleep	dream	fly	catch	throw	close (eyes)
attack	stab	run	away (flee)	help	shine (light)
drive	watch	burn	tell	look	release (let go)

2 The students should then take turns miming the verb list while their partner guesses the verbs.

3 Finally, they should make predictions, based on the verb list, about what they will see in the video.

VARIATION 1

After the students have made their predictions, some pairs may wish to share what they have predicted. You can tell them what really happens, using the vocabulary on the list.

VARIATION 2

You could give the students a list of nouns instead of verbs, and ask them to construct a story (see activity 4.1).

REMARKS

It is a good idea to note down the past tenses of the verbs if you plan to go on to activity 5.4.

5.4 Half n' half

LEVEL

Lower-intermediate to advanced

TIME

10 minutes

AIM

To practise the simple past and past continuous tenses with the vocabulary from activity 5.3 to describe what happened in the video.

PREPARATION

Before class, check that you know how to turn the sound off your video recorder. Arrange the seats so that only half the class can see the video, for example:

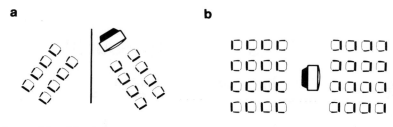

a

(movable video)

b

c

(fixed video)

d

IN CLASS

1 Ask the students to sit according to your pre-arranged pattern.

2 Explain that only half the class will be able to see the video.

3 Tell the half that can see the monitor that they will only see about 30 seconds of the video with no sound. Their job is to remember as much as possible of what they see so they can tell a partner from the other half what it was all about.
(The other half may find it amusing to observe the faces of those watching the video and to try to guess what is happening from their facial expressions. They should not turn around and look at the video.)

4 Show the video for about 30 seconds. Then tell the students to find someone from the half of the class that has not seen the video and to explain to them what happened. (They can use the verb list from activity 5.3 as a memory prompt.)

5 Change the groups around, and follow the same procedure for the next 30 seconds of the video.

6 When both halves of the class have had a chance to see the video and talk about it, you could move on to 5.5 or 5.10.

VARIATION

Those who were not looking should be encouraged to ask questions of those who were, and to get as much information as possible. You could prepare questions similar to the ones in activity 5.2 and either give them to the students or put them up on the board. The students then try to predict what will come next in the video.

REMARKS

A good lead-in to this activity is 5.3.

5.5   Hear all about it!

LEVEL

Intermediate to advanced

TIME

15 minutes

AIM

To practise the present continuous tense and vocabulary.

PREPARATION

For lower-level classes, choose a video that does not change frames too quickly. (With some videos, even native speakers have trouble keeping up with the pace of rapidly changing frames. But remember that you can usually use the pause button if it is going too fast for the group.)

IN CLASS

1 Put students into pairs and place one of each pair facing the video and the other looking at the first one's face.

2 Instruct the students facing the video to watch and describe to their partners what they see. They should concentrate on two things:
a. naming objects, for example *There's a man*, and
b. saying what someone is doing (*She's dancing/She's singing/She's running.*), using the vocabulary list from activity 5.3.

3 Play a short section of the video and stop it after 30 seconds or so. The students describe what they saw.

4 Ask the pairs to change over and repeat the process with another 30-second segment of the video.

VARIATION 1 The video can be run through several times. It is also fun and can be funny to run it backwards. The students should still try to say what they see.

VARIATION 2 The half of the class that has not seen the video can formulate a few questions for the other half to answer on the second showing. (For example, *How is the man dressed? What colour are his eyes? What's in the background when she's singing?*)

VARIATION 3 The half of the class listening to the other half can take down notes of everything they say. When the video stops, they reformulate: *At one point you said that they were running, and then falling, and then someone stabbed somebody . . .*

5.6 Guessing the music and song

LEVEL Lower-intermediate to advanced

TIME 10–15 minutes

AIM To practise prediction and guessing spoken context from visual clues.

PREPARATION Prepare a set of questions to hand out, to put on the board, or to ask orally. If you prepare the questions as a hand-out, make enough copies for half the class, and let pairs discuss them. For example:
– *Is the song fast or slow? (What makes you think so?)*
– *What kind of instruments do you think you will hear?*
– *What kind of voice will the singer have?*
– *Will we be able to understand the words?*
– *What will the lyrics be about?*
– *Is it a love song, a breaking-up song?* etc.

IN CLASS **1** Show a section of the video without the sound.

2 When the students have seen the video silently, they should have some idea what the song might be.

3 Put your list of questions on the board or give them out for the students to discuss in pairs or small groups.

4 Then allow the whole group to give their ideas before actually watching the video with the sound *on* this time.

REMARKS

This activity is a natural follow-on from 5.4 and 5.5.

5.7   Creating dialogues

LEVEL

Intermediate to advanced

TIME

10–45 minutes

AIM

To practise creating imaginary dialogues from visual clues.

PREPARATION

Find a video with a dramatic scene or a clear story-line in it.

IN CLASS

1 Stop the tape at four or five different places, with different people on the screen. Ask the students to write answers to the following questions:
– *What do you think this person is feeling/thinking/or saying?*

2 They compare their answers in small groups.

3 This can lead into an open discussion and the creation of a dialogue by the whole class.

VARIATION

An advanced class could write a script and story-line to accompany the silent video.

1 The students first write a draft, and adjust it as the video is shown.

2 When they have a polished version, the students act it out, with the video, either 'solo' or with several voices.

5.8   Guessing video from song text or audio tape

LEVEL

Intermediate to advanced

TIME

15 minutes

AIM

To practise the language of prediction.

PREPARATION

1 Prepare hand-outs of the lyrics for the song you have chosen.

2 If you feel you may want to use the text for 'exercises', prepare gap-fill, cloze, word change, or other exercise types with the text.

3 You will need to hand out the lyrics at some point, whether you begin with the music (song) or do the text-based Variation 1.

IN CLASS

1 Turn on the video recorder so that you have the sound but not the picture.

2 The students listen to the song once through to get a general impression. Ask them:
- *What kind of atmosphere is created by the music and vocals (even if you didn't understand the words)?*
- *What words did you understand?*
- *What do you know about the singer?*

3 Tell them you will play it once more. While it is playing, they should try to imagine how many people there are; what the images are like; what the setting is; how the images will change—quickly or slowly; whether the song is fast or slow, etc. (This will elicit the language of probability, such as *It must be . . . It probably looks . . .*, examples of which you could put on the board, depending on the level of your group.)

4 Ask the students to compare their predictions in small groups, and then to write a few of them on the board.

5 Then view the video.

6 After the viewing, ask students to compare what was written on the board with the video, for example, *Juan thought that it was going to be at night. Was it?* etc.

7 You could hand out the lyrics at this stage, if you wish.

VARIATION 1

1 Instead of beginning with the music, start with the lyrics (and no sound).

2 Hand out the lyrics and go over them with the students to check comprehension.

3 Tell the class they will then see the video, but first you want them to guess what they are going to see, based on the text. Ask them:
- *How many people do you think there will be?*
- *What images will be involved?*
- *What will the setting be?*
- *Will the images change quickly or slowly?*
- *Is the song fast or slow?* etc.

VARIATION 2

You could use the activity and Variation 1 to encourage the students to do some writing, using constructions like: *We thought there would be dancing (in the video), but there wasn't.*

5.9   Using the present perfect

LEVEL

Beginners to intermediate

TIME

10–20 minutes

AIM

To introduce, revise, or practise the present perfect tense.

PREPARATION

1 Choose a video suitable for the level of the class.

2 Watch the first half, then stop it. Prepare a set (see example below) of about ten questions, such as:
– *Have you seen a man singing yet?*
The questions should be in the present perfect, and about things that *are* in the video, and things that are *not*, for example:
– *Have you seen a pink elephant with a blue bow tie yet?*
Make enough copies for half the class.

3 Then look at the second half (to just before the end), and prepare another set of ten questions like the first, using the present perfect. Make enough copies for the other half of the class.

IN CLASS

1 As in 5.4, divide the class into two groups so that only one group can see the video screen.

2 Show the first part of the video (without sound) to one group. They should try to remember as much as possible because after the viewing they will have to explain to the other group what they saw.

3 The group that saw the video form pairs with students who did not.

4   When they have had time to describe what happened, those who did not see the video are given the first set of questions and told to ask their partners the questions.

5 Tell the partners to answer either *Yes, I have.* or *No, I haven't.* They can then enlarge on the answer, using the simple past.

6 When they have been through the questions, the two halves of the class change over, and the other half sees the second part of the video almost to the end.

7 Hand out the second set of questions to the non-viewing group, and repeat the procedure.

REMARKS

After each group has watched their half of the video, they will be describing what they saw in the simple past (if you follow the procedure in 5.4). Once they start asking questions from your list, they will be using only the present perfect tense, and then perhaps the simple past again if they explain in detail. For example, they might say *Yes, I have seen a boat. It was blue and had a tall mast.* This is a good opportunity to call attention to the different uses of these two tenses.

5.10 Using the past continuous

LEVEL

Intermediate to advanced

TIME

5–10 minutes

AIM

To practise using the past continuous tense.

PREPARATION

1 Prepare a set of questions in the past continuous (as if two people were trying to remember what was going on at certain times during the video), for example:
– *What was the singer doing the first time you saw him?*
– *What was X wearing when you first saw her?* etc.

2 Make enough copies for the whole class.

IN CLASS

1 As in activity 5.9, half the class sees the first half of a video and, later, the other half sees the rest.

2 When both groups have finished viewing their part, hand out the questions and put the students in pairs. The partners who each saw different parts of the video discuss their answers, using the past continuous questions on the hand-out and/or others of their own making.

5.11 Countdown exercise

LEVEL

All levels

TIME

5–10 minutes

AIM

To encourage listening for specific information.

PREPARATION

Video-record from a hit song TV programme a portion when the presenters are summarizing the position of the hit songs for that week. Announcers usually do this in tens, that is, they go from 40 to 31, 30 to 21, etc. and then they usually show a few video clips.

IN CLASS

1 Play the countdown once or twice through and then let the students get together in small groups to share their information and to home in on information they do not yet have.

2 Then play the clip again for the students to listen selectively for the information that they did not get the first time round.

3 Finally, ask members from the different groups to come up and write their information on the board. Discuss any discrepancies between the groups' findings.

4 Have a final viewing to settle any doubts!

VARIATION

1 Instead of forming small groups, each person can be assigned a different number in the countdown and asked to listen specifically for that number.

2 On the first showing you may wish to turn off either the picture, or the sound, so that the students are only monitoring one source of sensory input and gathering their information from that.

3 At a later stage, add the other mode (vision or sound), so that the students can gather further information.

REMARKS

1 At first this can be a very frustrating exercise because it is language at its fastest. Prepare the students and let them know they will hear it two or three times.

2 Also, depending on the announcer and the station, there can be more or less clarity, extra information, etc. The usual categories on their countdowns are: place, singer, song, place in the previous week (for example, up three places), and additional information.

3 Finally, for lower-level classes, it is important to make frequent use of the pause button.

5.12   Some know, some don't

LEVEL

Intermediate to advanced

TIME

15–30 minutes

AIM

To share expectations and information in an intriguing way.

PREPARATION

1 Choose a video clip suitable to the level of the class. You need to be reasonably sure that some have seen it and others have not. Usually a current number one hit will work but, to be sure, ask the students how many have/have not seen it a few classes before you plan to use it. A clip that has received a lot of publicity for some reason is usually ideal because it is controversial in some way. (I have used *Thriller* (Michael Jackson) and *Like a Prayer* (Madonna) this way. Below I use the example of *Like a Prayer*.)

2 Prepare the lyrics of the song for the whole class.

IN CLASS

1 In order to decide on grouping, ask:
– *Who has seen the clip 'Like a Prayer' by Madonna?*
Those who raise their hands move to one corner of the room. Then ask:
– *Who has heard about the clip from friends, or read about it in newspapers or magazines?*

Those who have this sort of information stand in another corner. Finally, those who know nothing about the clip and who have not seen it should stand in a third corner. Repeat the composition of the three groups and allow students to change groups if they had misunderstood what you meant:
- *Group A have seen the clip.*
- *Group B have not seen it, but have some information about it.*
- *Group C have neither seen nor heard about it.*

2 Instruct the first two groups (A and B) to compile information and to appoint a spokesperson to summarize what they know. Insist on a consensus on the version that this person is going to tell the rest of the class.

3 Give the lyrics of the song to group C and ask them to imagine what the video will be about, where will it take place, who will be in it, and what things will they see. Again, ask them to pool their impressions and to come to some agreement on what their spokesperson will tell the rest.

4 Allow sufficient time for them to get their ideas together.

5 Then ask group C (who have not seen the clip) to say what they think will be in the clip, based on their reading of the lyrics.

6 Then ask group B (who have not seen the clip, but have heard and read about it) to comment on the other group's imaginary clip, and to supply such information as they have.

7 Finally, group A (who have seen the clip) comment on, and perhaps correct, what was said by the other two groups and talk about what they remember of the clip. (The motivation to see the clip at this point is usually very high, owing to layered information and sheer curiosity!)

8 Show the clip in full at the end of the activity.

VARIATION 1

You could supply the second group with a relevant article to stimulate further interest and discussion.

VARIATION 2

When working with a more dated clip, divide the class into two groups only—those who have seen it and those who have not.

REMARKS

In any given class, either all, or none of the students will be familiar with a given video clip. When either all or none of the students know it, the activity is straightforward. There may seem to be a problem if some students know the video and others do not. But like so many so-called problems, such a situation can lead to more creative involvement from the participants and fuller use of the material. (This activity has worked so well for me in my classes that I have found myself wishing that the 'problem' arose more often than it does.)

5.13   Exploring socio-cultural symbols

LEVEL

Intermediate to advanced

TIME

Variable

AIM

To appreciate some of the finer 'literary' techniques involved in some videos and songs.

PREPARATION

1 Try to find a video which contains symbols and references. As yet there are no collections of pop song video clips for language teaching. Teachers are left more or less on their own to collect and analyse them with their students. In the context of this activity, I have used Michael Jackson's *Thriller* (in which the symbols are the American use of the car, dating and cars, running out of gas/ parking, the class ring, the leather jacket, going steady, and teenage wolfman/horror movies), David Bowie's *Day In Day Out* (with the symbolic angel, Marilyn Monroe, the American eagle, the video camera), and Madonna's *Like a Prayer* (with its crosses, Klu Klux Klan, female/black Jesus, and dancing in church).

2 Prepare a list of a few things you would like the students to focus on:
– *You will see a sort of angel holding something. You will also see an image of Marilyn Monroe. What do you think their connection with the song is?* (For David Bowie's *Day In, Day Out*.)
Musicals can also be used for this activity, for example, in *Mary Poppins* there is Mrs Banks' daily routine song (timing, slippers, paper, pipe) and Mrs Banks' suffragette song. (For more details on this musical see activity 5.18.)
In the Bibliography, I have listed several book collections of contemporary songs which are thematically organized for EFL instruction according to lyrical references and symbols.

IN CLASS

1 Write on the board a list of symbols that you have identified in the video.

2 Ask the students to look for them while watching the video, as they will be discussing their significance in small groups later.

3 Put on the video.

4 Let the students discuss the clip in relation to the symbols for five to ten minutes.

5 Advanced and multicultural groups may enjoy discussing how such symbols would be understood in their own culture.

REMARKS

1 When students comment on the symbolism, be prepared to accept any ideas, and avoid giving your own, unless solicited by the group. In this kind of activity, there are no right answers.

2 Some students may already be senstive to certain symbols. Once the others are, they seem to find them everywhere and it is no longer necessary to ask the students to search for them.

5.14   What makes a good video?

LEVEL   Lower-intermediate to advanced

TIME   30–50 minutes

AIM   To encourage students to practise the language of negotiation, and
                            to sensitize them to the opinions of others.

PREPARATION   As a warm-up to this exercise, discuss in a previous class what
                            makes a good video. Ask the students to discuss the questions in
                            pairs and to list all the things that they think makes a good video.
                            They hand in their criteria to you at the end of the class.

                            1 Type up a composite rating form like the one below, with two
                            forms on one sheet.

                            2 Make enough copies for the whole class.

**SAMPLE
QUESTIONNAIRE**

Video evaluation form
Song 1
How would you rate this video clip? 1 = very bad, not at all,
6 = very good, very much.

The song		*Notes*
The music	1 2 3 4 5 6	
The lyrics	1 2 3 4 5 6	
The voice	1 2 3 4 5 6	

The singer(s)
The look   1 2 3 4 5 6
Acting   1 2 3 4 5 6
Dancing   1 2 3 4 5 6

The clip
Special effects   1 2 3 4 5 6
Originality/creativity   1 2 3 4 5 6
Story-line   1 2 3 4 5 6
Costumes and make-up   1 2 3 4 5 6
Does the video remain faithful to the
song/ do they go well together? 1 2 3 4 5 6
Would you like to see it again? 1 2 3 4 5 6

Who do you think the target audience is?
Is there an important message? What is the purpose of the song and video? Is there any
emotional impact?

Overall score for song video 1 2 3 4 5 6
(Repeat for Song 2)

IN CLASS

1 Hand out the criteria-scoring sheet, and put the class into groups of four. Make sure the students understand all the categories, and ask if they want to add any others.

2 Then either show two videos that they have seen or two that they have not seen.

3 They have to score the two videos on a scale of 1–6, and to agree on their score or to compromise when they disagree.

4 Allow the students plenty of time for discussion if the activity is going well. If you notice that one group has finished, join them and ask them to explain their scoring to you, and at the same time tell the other groups that they should finish in just a few minutes.

5 When all the groups have finished, put up a grid on the board for the two clips, and ask for the overall scores for each video from the different groups as you write them on the board.

Group	Song 1	Song 2
1		
2		
3		
4		

6 Sometimes groups attribute very different scores. When this happens, you can ask the groups concerned to explain why their scores are different. This is one of the best features of the exercise, since it enables students to see how differently they perceive the same things. It also encourages a good deal of language interaction in a task-based context.

VARIATION

For homework, students could write an essay comparing the two videos, and identifying what they think makes a good video clip. They could also report the different opinions of the groups.

5.15   Making video clips

LEVEL

All levels

TIME

Part of several classes (and possibly extra-curricular time)

AIM

To use the target language while planning and writing a script, practising, and filming it.

PREPARATION

1 Obtain a video camera, video cassette recorder, and monitor, and ensure you know how to use them. You will also need to instruct your camera operator.

2 Prepare enough copies of the options sheet below for the whole class.

SAMPLE HAND-OUT

Making a video clip: options

1 We film you acting out a song with the original sound track in the background. This merely requires you to write the screenplay and camera directions, and can be done with a song or instrumental music. We would start with this and then follow it up with any of the options below.

2 You peform the song as well.

3 Or you rewrite the words of a known song, making the words specific to a particular situation (for example, school or political life).

4 You write your own songs, words, and music.

5 You organize a mini-musical in which one or two songs are embedded in a narrative with dialogue, along the lines of *Thriller*.

6 You interview a well-known person, and make their response to each question part of a song.

7 You make a pop TV show in which you interview stars (made-up or real) and show their clips.

8 You set up a talent show and film it.

9 You film familiar people at the school (teachers and students) doing things, and then dub songs over their action (for example, film the director of the school speaking and record over it *Words don't come easy to me ...*).

10 You record famous people on TV for at least 30 seconds. Then choose songs that would accompany them in a humorous way.

11 You integrate songs and video into project work (using subjects such as drugs, apartheid, etc.).

12 We choose a well-known song and you write a scenario in the way a film producer might, dividing the page into three columns for lyrics, action, and on camera. Then you all work together on it.

IN CLASS

1 Ask your students if they would like to make a pop song video. (If they are not very motivated, abandon the activity—it requires a lot of persistence, hard work, and enthusiasm on their part.) Let them know that it will require a lot of work, but that it is also fun.

2 Hand out the list of options to consider.

3 After they have chosen one of the options, students need to plan it first on paper. The easiest way to do this is to divide a page into three columns:

Making a video	Song:_____	
Words	Action	Camera directions

4 The students then list all the materials they need and all the work that needs to be done.

5 Then they volunteer for the different jobs. All the students should help in writing and planning, but the class will need to appoint specific people to act, sing, play instruments, film, record the sound, organize props, lighting, find documents, get permissions, etc. If there are jobs that no one is willing to do, replan the activity so that you can do it without them.

6 After the filming, the class might want to add a soundtrack or mix the video with other things. And, of course, they will want to organize a grand première and to invite special guests!

VARIATION

Large classes can divide themselves into groups and explore different options.

REMARKS

This activity *is* labour-intensive and time-consuming. However, when the students are really engaged in it, they get immense satisfaction from their own creativity and, of course, the reward of viewing their own creation afterwards.

5.16   Using an outline

LEVEL   All levels

TIME   Variable

AIM   To practise retelling dialogues in narrative form using a prompt sheet.

PREPARATION 1 Prepare a hand-out such as the one below (based on *Thriller*) listing most of the verbs and vocabulary to tell the story.

2 Make enough copies for the whole class.

IN CLASS   1 Give the hand-out to the students.

2 Explain what is going to happen in the video. Use mainly the words on the hand-out and let the students follow the clip.

3 After the students have watched the video, put them in pairs and ask them to retell the story in the past tense.

VARIATION 1 1 Put the class into small groups.

2 Ask those students who have seen the clip to explain it to those who have not, using the outline as support. (See activity 5.12.)

VARIATION 2 1 Show half the class the video, while the other half does another activity out of the room. Give the group watching the video the outline and help them to tell the story to a partner from the other group.

2 Pair them all up when the other group comes back. The other group must also be given the opportunity to share the task they carried out outside the classroom (for example, the construction of a music questionnaire).

REMARKS   The outline can also be used for summarizing a video, writing a review, or a critical analysis, or for preparing for a test.

'Thriller' video skeleton

Verbs	Past tense	Vocabulary
First frame		
be, stop		night, old car (convertible), out of gas, boy and girl, with old clothes, in it
walk		through the forest (woods)
stop		
talk		each other
tell		'I love you'
ask		'be my girl'
kiss and hug		each other
give		ring
confess		not normal boy
see		full moon
turn into (become)		wolfman
scream		
chase		girl
Change of frame		(To cinema)
watch		movie/film
be (scared), excuse		
leave		theatre
walk		(Song starts)
sing		
dance		
walk		by graveyard
come to life		zombies
they follow		boy and girl
surround		them
change/transform		boy into zombie
dance		(Song ends)
chase		girl
run		to abandoned haunted house
screams		(Music stops)
Change of frame		
wake up		
take home		

(American cultural concepts: parking/running out of gas, dating/driving cars, leather jacket, going steady, class ring.)

6 With young children

The activities in this section are really for students of all ages, although they may be more frequently used with small children. In many ways, children are the easiest students to use music and song with. When children sing, they seem completely uninhibited, as if suddenly and magically they forget to be shy. They become the word they sing, as their bodies move and their voices leap to express their feelings. Repetition seems never to bore them although it may sometimes drive teachers crazy!

This section will probably have little that is new for teachers who are already experienced early-education professionals. There is in most languages a wealth of materials for young children. These materials are often quite suitable for the EFL class. (See Bibliography.) Even as long ago as 1943 there were collections of finger play songs, echo songs, refrain songs, question and answer songs, movement and physical training songs, mime songs, speech training songs, pitch songs, 'topic' songs, lullabies, and spirituals.

This section starts with warm-up techniques for eventual singing (shouting, repeating, backward formations), then presents jazz chants (rhythm without a singing melody), and finally presents different song-types, the most important being Total Physical Response (TPR) or action songs.

Jazz chants were made popular by Carolyn Graham (see Bibliography) and are much easier and often more fun for children than actual songs (and also for teachers who may lack confidence in their singing). They consist of time-stressed phrases of certain lengths that can be tapped out, with foot, hand, or pencil. They are amazingly simple to write, and you can target the vocabulary and expressions to your particular students. Even students can write them themselves with relative ease. Try your own hand at them!

The age-old technique of asking students to perform actions with words was first described as Total Physical Response (TPR) by James Asher (1965). Since then it has become even more popular because of well-documented research that shows it to be very effective. The idea is that if students can move and do what is said (either by someone else or themselves) matching words to the actions, language is learnt more deeply. It is encoded kinesthetically as well as through the ears and eyes. With young children, language divorced from action seems to be mostly forgotten.

With some TPR songs, the students are merely asked to move—they sing only when they are ready. The music ties words and

motion together, and increases memorability. The music allows
students to be silent, yet still to show comprehension through their
actions. Later, when the songs come to be sung, they are sung in
group discourse, hence putting no individual too much in the
limelight. TPR allows students to have their silent period as
advocated by Krashen (1985).

Activities from other sections of this book that work particularly
well with children include all of Section 2 and many of the activites
from the other sections, provided the task and the language are
adjusted to the children's level.

6.1   TPR shouting up/down

LEVEL	**Beginners to advanced**
TIME	**5 minutes**
AIM	To help students to discover their voices and to overcome the fear of saying things in a foreign language.
PREPARATION	None.
IN CLASS	**1** Ask the class to stand in a circle, and point up, saying *up*. Do the same with *down*, then combine them. Let them repeat and do the actions with you, first softly and then loudly, then shouting. (They may be shocked at first, but then they enjoy being able to let go a little.)
	2 Then do the motions and get the students to say the words without you. This can be done with several different actions, instructions, and indications.
EXAMPLES	(pointing to and combining the objects or concepts in various ways) Up/down Left/right Front/back Cheek/chin/chest

3 A fun jazz chant to do is the children's verse *I scream*. Children
are already familiar with the international term *ice-cream*, so it is
enough to teach them *scream* which is easily illustrated. You can
illustrate the personal pronouns with arm gestures. While singing/
shouting it is fun to start very softly and then get louder and louder.
You can do it like a jazz chant:
I scream
You scream
We all scream
For **ice**-cream.

4 You can get the students to respond to various objects (or pictures) that you hold up. Students shout *I like* it and *I don't like* it (with stress and extra-special emphasis) in response to pictures of food items, or they may say the names of sports as you show them different items of equipment.

REMARKS

This activity is best done in a well sound-proofed room. Those in the vicinity may have to be warned that you will occasionally be doing a shouting exercise. I had one administrator ask me what all the arguing was about in my last class, as he had heard us shouting (he thought) at each other.

6.2   Chorus back-chaining

LEVEL

All levels

TIME

5–10 minutes

AIM

To increase confidence in pronunciation through learning to say long words.

PREPARATION

None.

IN CLASS

1 When you hear students having difficulty getting their tongue around a long word or sentence, try getting them to pronounce it in segments, from the end backwards. Ask them to repeat the last syllable with you, then the last two plus the middle one, then the last two again, then the last four.

2 Repeat the following and ask your students to repeat after each:

EXAMPLE

Supercalifragilisticexpiallidocious

Su per cal i fra gil is tic	is–tic
ex pi al li do cious	fra–gil
do–cious	fra–gil–is–tic
al–li–do–cious	cal–i
ex–pi	Su–per–cal–i
ex–pi–al–li	fra–gil–is–tic
al–li–do–cious	Su–per–cal–i–fra–gil–is–tic (x 3)
ex–pi–al–li–do–cious (x3)	Su per cal i fra gil is tic
	ex pi al li do cious (x3)

3 Repeat as many times as necessary the parts that cause difficulty. At the end they may still stumble a bit. Singing the line is somehow easier than just speaking it.

4 The students can then say it in pairs or small groups at their own pace.

VARIATION

If you want the students to practise it at home, tell them that they must answer with the whole word when you do the roll call the following day. (You could also do this with activities in 6.1.)

REMARKS

Try not to be shy about trying this with older students. It still works. As a reward, if you have the *Mary Poppins* video or song on cassette, play it to the students and let them chant along with it.

6.3   Jazz chants

LEVEL

All levels

TIME

5 minutes

AIM

To practise syllable stress, enunciation, intonation; to have fun.

PREPARATION

1 Find or write a jazz chant (see Graham 1978) that is suitable to the age and level of your students. Practise it yourself so that you know how it feels to say it. You may also want to test teach it to colleagues and get their feedback.

2 Prepare hand-outs with the words (for students who are of reading age). If you type the words on a word processor, you can make the stressed syllables **bold** to **make** it **ea**sier to **see** which **ones** should be **stressed**. <u>O</u>therwise simply <u>un</u>derline the <u>stressed words.</u>

IN CLASS

1 Let the students tap with their hands, feet, or pencil to keep the rhythm. Chant it out once as they just tap and read or listen.

2 Then go through the chant line by line until the students get the gist of it, but do not insist on perfection!

3 Gradually build up to two lines and then the whole chant.

4 Once the students have been through it all once, stop and explain the meanings of the words if they are not clear (very often the meanings will slowly dawn on the students if they are simply allowed to handle the words in a playful manner as with a chant).

5 Then chant it again, dividing up the class into two groups.

VARIATION   Let pairs of students work by themselves alternating the different parts. However, all the pairs should do this at once, as it is often too embarrassing for one pair to do it in front of the class. Even so, it is hilarious when you have fifteen or twenty pairs of students doing the chant to the beat of their own drums!

REMARKS   After doing the chant below, I get them to describe their routine to their partners. The one who is listening is told to respond each time their partner pauses with *And then what? What next?* very quickly. This is a discourse game and the students have a lot of fun with it. They follow it up with a written description of their own daily routine. If they are feeling creative, encourage them to try to make it into a short jazz chant of their own.

SAMPLE HAND-OUT

My usual routine

One	*Two*	*One*	*Two*
When **I** get **up** I **make** my **bed** I **clean** my **room** and **brush** my **teeth**,		After **din**ner I **might** go **danc**ing See a **film** Or **talk** to **friends**,	
	And **then what**? **What next**?		And **then what**? **What next**?
I **have** my **break**fast **Go** and do **sports** play **lots** of **games** have **lots** of **fun**,		I'll **take** a **show**er **Brush** my **teeth** **Go** to **bed** and **have** sweet **dreams**,	
	And **then what**? **What next**?		And **then what**? **What next**?
After **lunch** I **might** go **hik**ing I **might** go **sail**ing or **may**be **skat**ing,		**That**'s e**nough** **Don't** you **think** And **what** about **you** **What** about **you**?	
	And **then what**? **What next**?		Oh **I'm** too **lazy** **Much** too **tired** **Thanks** all the **same** **Thanks** all the **same**.

6.4   TPR hiking jazz chants

LEVEL

All levels

TIME

15 minutes

AIM

To teach the two meanings of *left* and *right*, to make students aware of their kinesthetic difference, and to have fun (on hikes and excursions).

PREPARATION

Make photocopies of the following example.

EXAMPLE

Hiking jazz chant

One	*Two*
Left, left	
Left, right, left	
I **left** my **room** in a **mess.**	
	You're **right**.
I **left** my **socks** in the **sink.**	
	You're **right**.
	You're **right**.
	You're **right, left, right.**
	Sing out!
One two	
	(All together)
	One, two, three, four, one, two.

IN CLASS

1 First teach left and right directions. Then, while sitting, teach the students to march with their hands on the tops of the tables or desks. If you demonstrate it for them, make sure you do it with your back to them so as not to confuse them. That way they see your left as their left!

2 Hand-march through the jazz chant once. Then explain the different meanings of the words *left, right, mess,* etc. Let the students sing it several times through with you. (Do not pound your hands too hard, they get sore!)

3 Divide the class, one half saying *One*, and the other *Two*, and all of them doing the last line.

4 When everybody has got it, ask the class to stand up and do marching in place, first as a group; then individual pairs do it to their own beat. Help them out with problems when needed.

VARIATION

Take a hike through the school hall or outside (at break) while chanting it.

6.5 Action songs

LEVEL

Children (or mature adults who do not mind being childlike)

TIME

10 minutes (at the beginning of a class; two minutes when repeated at the end of a class)

AIM

To teach the vocabulary of parts of the body (head, shoulders, knees, and toes).

PREPARATION

1 Learn the song yourself.

2 Prepare any necessary hand-outs. (Other suitable songs for this activity are listed below. Teachers and children can make up different words to these songs if they want to.)

IN CLASS

1 Ask the students to repeat lines, or parts of lines, after you, while touching the relevant part of the body (or performing the actions). When they are familiar with the actions, sing the song *Head, shoulders, knees and toes* through once, encouraging them to do the actions as you do them.

Head, shoulders, knees and toes, knees and toes
and eyes and ears and mouth and nose
Head, shoulders, knees and toes, knees and toes.

2 Repeat the song. The students should sing more as you fade out. But be ready to come back in if and when needed.

REMARKS

1 TPR songs can also be used as pseudo-tests. I sing *If you're happy and you know it, touch your ear* and by their response I find out what they know. After they know the song I can vary other words *If you're crazy and you know it, clap your hands*, etc.

2 Often there are several tunes or lyrical variations to the same children's song as a result of being passed down through oral tradition. (Songs change like languages!) Do not tell a child or teacher that their version is wrong it they sing a different one from you. Learn it their way and make a friend!

SAMPLE MATERIALS

Songs for TPR
1 This is the way we wash our hands, we wash our hands, we wash our hands.
   This is the way we wash our hands, early in the morning.
   (comb our hair, bounce a ball, kick, etc.) (to the tune of *Here we go round the Mulberry Bush*)
2 If you're happy and you know it, clap your hands
   If you're happy and you know it, clap your hands
   If you're happy and you know it, and you really want to know it
   If you're happy and you know it, clap your hands.
   (stomp your feet, shout hooray, do all three, etc.)
3 My hat it has three feathers, three feathers has my hat
   And had it not three feathers, it would not be my hat.

4 Swing low sweet chariot, coming for to carry me home
   Swing low sweet chariot, coming for to carry me home
   I looked over Jordan and what did I see
   Coming for to carry me home
   A band of angels coming after me
   Coming for to carry me home.
   Swing low sweet chariot . . .

   (Actions include: swinging low, bowing low, and swinging your
   arms on the words *Swing low*; kissing your fingertips on the word
   sweet; holding reins of horse; motioning someone to come;
   folding arms in front like holding a baby; pointing to self/making
   a roof over your head with hands and arms as in looking (like an
   Indian shielding eyes); making a wavy motion like the sea;
   playing the trumpet/flapping your elbows like wings; and making
   a *come here* sign.)
5 John Jacob Jingle Heimer Smith, his name is my name too (3,4,5)
   Whenever we go out, the people always shout, there goes
   John Jacob Jingle Heimer Smith, DADADADADADADA
   (words softer each time while always shouting DADADA).
6 Other songs
   *Ten Little Indians, Brother John, My Marvellous Little Toy, Hokey
   Pokey, Kumbaya*, and any ones you care to choose.

6.6 Repetition songs

LEVEL

All levels

TIME

5 minutes (at the beginning of a class)

AIM

To reinforce pronunciation through song.

PREPARATION

Learn the songs yourself or try out a cassette version. Think of
possible ways of illustrating them. You might also think of
substitute words and phrases, for example, instead of *Ten Little
Indians*, change it to *Ten Little Puppies*; instead of *Here we go round
the Mulberry Bush*, why not use the things that your students do in
their own environment?

Examples of suitable songs are:
*One Little Indian, Old Macdonald; Hole in the bottom of the Sea; This
is the Way we Wash our Face* (to the tune of *Here we go round the
Mulberry Bush*).

IN CLASS

1 Teach the song. There are many different ways of teaching a
song. Most teachers, however, seem to like to either sing/play the

song completely through once to allow students to hear it all. Then they say or sing it a bit by bit with students repeating. Finally, they sing the whole song again.

2 Once the students have learnt it, give out parts and add actions.

3 Finally, if you are using them, hand out written texts. These can be illustrated, coloured, and exploited in transfer exercises.

REMARKS

Repetition songs are fun and help students to get hold of some of the language, but they are not enough in themselves. Words in the songs do not automatically transfer into use. For this we need transfer exercises to activate what has only been grasped in one way. For example, after teaching *Ten Little Indians*, you might count other objects in the room and do easy maths. To get the most out of songs, you can choose them either because they reinforce what is being learnt or exploit whatever content they offer beyond simply singing for itself.

6.7 Role-play songs

LEVEL

All levels

TIME

Variable

AIM

To contextualize vocabulary and make the transfer from singing to meaningful referents.

PREPARATION

Find a song which can be acted out and which has a narrative with different roles. Many TPR songs can be acted out, but are not really narrative and do not have roles (*If You're Happy*, etc.). Probably the most famous among teachers and children is *The Bear Song*, which exists in many versions. (See my version at the end of this activity.)

IN CLASS

1 There are two ways of using such a song:
a. Pre-teach the story, explain what happens, then teach the song.
b. Begin by teaching the song as an introduction and tell the story afterwards. You might want to experiment with both ways.

2 When you do the song, assign the roles and ask the students to act out what happens in the song at the appropriate places.

VARIATION 1

Students can write the story themselves following the singing and illustrate it with a drawing to reinforce it.

VARIATION 2

Students can perform it in a school meeting for other students, for parents, etc.

The bear song

To be acted out with a lead singer, a bear, and a tree (or perhaps a forest) with the audience repeating and joining in.

Lead   (Others repeat)
One day I went
into the woods
and there I met
a great big bear
(Repeat)

He looked at me
I looked at him
He sized me up
I sized up him
(Repeat)

He said to me
Why don't you run
I see you ain't
got any gun
(Repeat)

I said to me
that's a good idea
So come on feet
let's get out of here
(Repeat)

And so I ran
away from there
But right behind
me was that bear
(repeat)

Ahead of me
I saw a tree
Oh glory be
a great big tree
(Repeat)

The lowest branch
was ten feet up
I had to jump,
to trust my luck
(Repeat)

And so I jumped
into the air
but I missed that branch
a way up there
(Repeat)

Now don't you fret
and don't you frown
Cause I caught that branch
on my way down
(Repeat)

That's all there is
there ain't no more
Because my tongue
is getting sore.

6.8   Drop-a-word songs

LEVEL   **All levels**

TIME   **5–10 minutes**

AIM   To encourage internalization of language.

PREPARATION   Find a song with a steady rhythm, a catchy tune, and which can easily be mimed (see the example below).

EXAMPLE   A popular children's song of this sort is *My Hat it has Three Corners* (or *Feathers*), (*Mon Chapeau Il a Trois Plumes/Mein Hut der Hat Drei Ecken*). This starts out as a TPR song in which actions accompany the words. Gradually the words are left out, and only the actions remain. (Everyone has to sing internally in order to get the actions right.) The code of the actions is the following: 1 = my (hand on chest); 2 = hat (hand on head); 3 = three (show three fingers); 4 = corners (hand on elbow); 5 = negative verb (shake finger *no, no*).

My hat it has three corners
1 2   3   4

Three corners has my hat
 3   4   1 2

And had it not three corners
        5   3   4

It would not be my hat.
        5   1 2

IN CLASS

1 Sing the song once on your own with all the actions.

2 Then sing a few words at a time with the actions. Ask the students to repeat after you. Then try it again line by line.

3 Finally, sing the whole song a couple of times through.

4 After they have learnt the song and the actions, the students sing it again but leave out the word *my*, and just perform the action. Then they sing it again, this time leaving out *my* and *hat*, and so on until they have eliminated the four main words. At the end, it can be fun to try to sing it (or to mime it, rather) all the way through, without any words.

REMARKS

1 Song is, to a certan extent, like egocentric speech (Piaget). It is an external manifestation which can become more powerful if we internalize it. When children lose egocentric speech, they learn that the words in their minds do not have to be spoken to exist—they can just think them. Just 'thinking' the words without singing them may encourage this process of internalization and encourage our inner voices to play silently with language.

2 When children and adults learn a song, it is not easy to leave words out immediately without some replacement action.

6.9 Class cassette

LEVEL

All levels

TIME

Parts of several classes

AIM

To reinforce the songs and language students have learnt.

PREPARATION

1 Plan the number of songs you wish to record, and the order of recording. These should be ones that you have already learnt with your class. Sometimes you may wish to record several sessions and then choose those selections that worked out well and mix them on a master tape.

2 Think about introductions and speaking/singing/sound effects parts for all the students.

3 Find the best tape recorder and microphone available. Often a simple cassette player will be good enough.

4 Buy enough cheap 45–60 minute cassettes for the whole class.

5 You can design the cassette labels and inserts yourself, or let your students do it. (In 1989, I did the one below and then let the children colour it as they wished.) You can photocopy the original that you make, then let the children cut them out and paste them on the inserts that come with the blank cassettes, for durability.

Done in the English classes August 1989

INTERNATIONAL SUMMER CAMP MONTANA

This cassette belongs to...

IN CLASS

1 Record the collection of songs with your students. Depending on their ability, and how many you have, you may wish to give each one 'centre stage' at least once during the recordings. Students (and parents!) are more motivated to listen to the cassette when they recognize their own/their children's voices. It is also probably clearer if there are only one, two, or three voices singing each verse. (Advanced students can sing the longer songs with lots of words, while the lower levels can sing the TPR songs and give short introductions written by them beforehand.)

2 After the recording, make copies of the cassette out of class (or give them to a language lab technician to make multiple copies). When each child is given a cassette, they colour the cassette label and put their name on it.

3 There may also be enough room at the end of each cassette for the teacher(s) and/or administrator(s) to record a personal message to each student.

VARIATION 1

Other things might be included on the cassette, such as a funny short story, jokes, interviews, and jazz chants.

VARIATION 2	You could make it like a radio show, with a mixture of songs, publicity spots, interviews, and disc-jockey chatter.
VARIATION 3	You and/or the students could also create a booklet to go along with the cassette (see activity 6.10).
REMARKS	**1** Although it sounds like an expensive venture, the material costs (the cassette) per student are minimal. However, they are also probably much more useful and used by students after the course than their coursebook! Administrators are sometimes willing to fund the project since it is also good publicity for the school.
	2 The cassettes are so popular that you sometimes get requests from other students and staff for copies.

6.10   Class songbook

LEVEL	**All levels**
TIME	**Throughout the year**
AIM	For students to produce a lasting record of their activities and creativity.
PREPARATION	There are three basic options in the creation of a class songbook.
	1 You know the songs that you want to do with the children. You copy and collate them at the beginning of the course. Then you work through the collection during the course, allowing the students to write and colour it as you work through it.
	2 You prepare a song folder that students use for copies of songs from you. (They may also include songs of their own choice from magazines or written in their own hand.) Ideally, at the end of the year you help them to put it into a more permanent form, perhaps with a cover page.
	Each time you hand out a new song, ask the students to file it in their song holder.
	3 Near the end of the course, give the students a written version of the songs that they may only have learnt orally during the course.
VARIATION	The class can record all or some of the songs on a cassette. (See activity 6.9.)
REMARKS	Such songbooks (and cassettes) can be made for special occasions like Christmas holidays, a school play, or around a theme (a mini *Live Aid* concert, for Amnesty International, etc.).

Appendix

1 Songs: academic and grammatical categories

Academic goals

Approaching the use of music and song from the point of view of academic goals can sometimes be artificial. With too much emphasis on practising the progressive or other grammatical constructions, some made-for-EFL materials have created song monstrosities of doubtful communicative content and devoid of the fun and excitement which full-bred commercial music and song use to engage listeners naturally.

Much better than starting with grammatical structures and writing songs to fit them, in my opinion, is starting from songs that the students are deeply interested in and seeing what can be learnt from them. Failing that, if we do wish to emphasize a certain structure, we can usually find commercially viable materials among the huge stock available. However, if we want writing, reading, listening, or discussion practice, nearly any song can offer a wide range of possibilities.

As far as addressing the four skill areas of reading, writing, listening, and speaking is concerned, many of the materials discussed in the preceding sections do this. The degree to which any of these skills is emphasized depends more upon the teacher's desired focus than the activity or song. We might call an activity like gap-fill a listening exercise, but the students all do reading and writing while completing the task. They may also discuss their answers with their neighbours.

Grammatical categories

Because most songs use a variety of tenses and grammatical structures, it is difficult to divide them up this way. Nevertheless, it is still attractive to our pedagogical agendas to try. Dubin (1974) offers an alternative when she suggests splitting them up into broader categories such as repetition songs (*Turn Turn Turn, Let It Be*), substitution songs (*Where Have All the Flowers Gone?, If I Had a Hammer*) and focused grammatical songs (for example, *El Condor Pasa*). Her last category brings us back to our desire to have a song that focuses principally on one grammatical point. The list below is for this third category. You should add to the list your own songs or those your students bring to you. Again, most songs use a variety of tenses and their listing here merely refers to a predominant tense.

The symbols beside the songs means that they can be found
in the following EFL songbooks:

♦ in *If You Feel Like Singing*
■ in *Sing It!*
+ in *Songs of Our Time*
□ in *Even If You Can't Carry a Tune*
⋆ in *Rock- und Popsongs im Englischunterricht*
– available in most commercial markets.

Present
♦ *You Are My Sunshine*
■ *My Bonnie*
■ *He's Got the Whole World*
■ *When the Saints Go Marching In*
□ *Little Boxes*
– *Let It Be* (The Beatles)

Continuous/progressive
■ *Are You Sleeping?* (Brother John)
□ *Oh What a Beautiful Morning*
+ *Sailing* (Rod Stewart)

Simple past
♦ *Yankee Doodle*
■ *Yesterday*
■ *Banks of the Ohio*
■ *Oh Suzanna!*
□ *The Marvellous Toy*

Past continuous
□ *Tennessee Waltz*

Present perfect
+ ⋆ *Streets of London*
♦ *Where Have All the Flowers Gone?*

Present perfect continuous
♦ *I've Been Workin' on the Railroad*
Abraham, Martin, and John (Marvin Gay)

Past perfect
■ *Last Night I Had The Strangest Dream* (by Ed McCurdy sung by
Simon and Garfunkel)

Future
♦ ■ *She'll Be Comin' Round the Mountain*
♦ *We Shall Overcome*
♦ *What Shall We Do with the Drunken Sailor?*

Modals
– *Blowing in the Wind* (Bob Dylan)

Imperatives
– *You Can Leave Your Hat On* (Joe Cocker)
– *Leaving on a Jet Plane* (John Denver)

Conditionals
- ♦ *If I Had a Hammer*
- – *El Condor Pasa*
- – ■ *With a Little Help from My Friends* (The Beatles)

Prepositions
- ■ *There's a Hole in the Bottom of the Sea*

Questions
Blowing in the Wind
Streets of London
Where Have all the Flowers Gone?
What have I done to deserve this? (Pet Shop boys)
Who's that Girl? (Madonna)

2   Songs: contemporary thematic categories

Many teachers find it useful to use songs to introduce themes for discussion or to reinforce other areas that have been studied. In this section I have also added in a few video clips (VC) where I have found them particularly appropriate.

Work
- + Billy Joel, *Allentown*
- + John Lennon, *Working Class Hero*
- + Eric Bogle, *No Use for Him*
- + Judy Collins, *Deportee*
- – Bruce Springsteen, *The River*
- (VC) Billy Joel, *Pianoman*

City life
- + Cat Stevens, *New York Times*
- + ⋆ Elvis Presley, *In the Ghetto*
- + Simon and Garfunkel, *The Sound of Silence*
- ⋆ Simon and Garfunkel, *The Boxer*
- Joni Mitchell, *Big Yellow Taxi*
- (VC) David Bowie, *Day In Day Out*
- (VC) Michael Jackson, *Beat It*
- (VC) Lou Reed, *Dirty Boulevard*

Modern times
- + Bob Dylan, *The Times They Are A-Changin'*
- + UB 40, *I Am the One in Ten*
- + Manfred Mann, *Lies* (through the 80s)
- + Wizz Jones, *Planet without a Plan*
- + Joan Baez, *Children of the Eighties*
- ⋆ Cat Stevens, *Where do the Children Play?*
- ⋆ America, *A Horse with no Name*
- (VC) Michael Jackson, *The Man in the Mirror*

Loneliness
+ Simon and Garfunkel, *I am a Rock, America*
+ The Beatles, *Eleanor Rigby*
+ Ralph McTell, *The Streets of London*
- Police, *Message in a Bottle*
- Don McLean, *Vincent*

Escape
+ Bert Jansch, *Needle of Death*
+ The Rolling Stones, *Mother's Little Helper*
+ Marianne Faithfull, *The Ballad of Lucy Jordan*
+ Rupert Holmes, *Escape*
- The Beatles, *She's Leaving Home*
(VC) Freddy Mercury, *The Great Pretender*

Love and friendship
+ Christopher Jones, *The Nightingale Song*
+ Kris Kristofferson, *Me and Bobby McGee*
+ Carole King, *You've Got a Friend*
⋆ The Beatles, *When I'm Sixty Four*
- Dan Fogelberg, *Same Auld Lang Syne*
(VC) Jason Donovan, *Sealed With A Kiss*

War and peace
+ Tom Paxton, *My Son John*
+ The Sands Family, *All the Little Children*
+ John Lennon, *Imagine*
- Simon and Garfunkel, *The Strangest Dream*
- Bruce Springsteen, *War*
- Bob Dylan, *A Hard Rain's A-Gonna Fall*

Leaving
■ *The Cruel War*
- John Denver, *Leaving on a Jet Plane*
- Jason Donovan, *Sealed With a Kiss*
⋆ The Beatles, *She's Leaving Home*
♦ Cat Stevens, *Father and Son*

Being a woman
- Janis Ian, *At Seventeen*
- Donna Summer, *I Will Survive*
- Suzanne Vega, *My Name is Luka*
- Tracy Chapman, *Behind the Wall*
- Helen Reddy, *I am Woman*
- Sheena Easton, *Modern Girl, Nine to Five*
- John Lennon, *Woman is the Nigger of the World*

Drugs
- John Lennon, *Cold Turkey*
- The Beatles, *Lucy in the Sky with Diamonds*
- Neil Young, *The Needle and the Damage Done*
- The Jefferson Airplane, *White Rabbit*
⋆ The Rolling Stones, *Mother's Little Helper*

Education
- Pink Floyd, *Another Brick in the Wall* (and the film)
- Alice Cooper, *School's Out*
- Crosby, Stills, Nash, and Young, *Teach Your Children*
- Boomtown Rats, *I don't like Mondays*

Racism
- Johnny Clegg, Asimbonoga, *Third World Child*
- Paul McCartney and Michael Jackson, *Ebony and Ivory*
- Genesis, *Illegal Alien*
(VC) Madonna, *Like a Prayer*

Make your own categories as the times develop and different social issues come to the forefront.

3   Magazines for lyrics to current songs, articles, and photos

EMAP Frontline
Park House 117 Park Road
Peterborough PE1 2TR
England

Smash Hits
Dept. SM484
Division St.
Derby CT 06418
USA

Hit Parader
P.O. Box 158
60 Division St.
Derby CT 06418
USA

Star Hits
PO Box 329
Mt. Morris, IL 61054
USA

TOP 50
(French and English songs)
99 rue d'Amsterdam
75008 Paris
France
Tel. 42 80 68 55

TOP Schlägertextheft
(often German translations of top European hits)
Musikverlag Hans Sikorski
2000 Hamburg 13
Germany

For play and sales charts plus music business news
Music & Media
European Music Report
PO Box 50558
1007 DB Amsterdam
The Netherlands

Made for EFL
I love English (France)
Bayard Presse S.A.
3–5 rue Bayard
75008 Paris Cedex
France

4   Case history of a pop video in the classroom

Sealed with a Kiss – SWAK

Jason Donovan recorded this old hit again for the summer of 1989 and it went to number one in June. I had recorded the video clip, so I simply wrote out the song and drew two little envelopes, a back and a front, below the words. On the back I wrote SWAK and drew some lips. In class, we briefly went over the lyrics so that they understood them and the idea of sealing your love letters with a kiss and writing SWAK. Then we watched the video, which was simple and easy to use for description.

After the students had seen it once, I asked them memory questions:
How many surfboards did you see?
What colour were the singer's eyes? etc.
Most couldn't answer and there were lots of guesses. So I told them I would show it again and asked them to look for these details, but also to look for others, and to think of one detail question they could ask the other students. They were much more attentive to detail the second time we saw it and enjoyed trying to make questions that the other students (and I!) couldn't answer. (*What colour were his shoelaces?*)

I then asked the students to write stereotypical love letters in pairs. They could write as if they were either the boy in the song or the girl. I asked them to use as many clichés as possible. They loved doing it and we discovered a lot of new and useful vocabulary that they were able to use.

Later I wrote a series of short letters, an exchange between a boy and girl, that told a story with the cliché that they had originally thought of, but varying it stylistically to get more and more intense, ending with a 'Dear John' letter breaking off the relationship. They had comprehension questions on the story afterwards. They enjoyed this because it was a mushy love story with a surprise ending.

Finally, I suggested the students write secret love letters to staff in the camp. Again, they were to have a lot of fun and use a lot of clichés. They would sign the letter with a code name and ask the staff members to reply by putting a letter in my mail box, addressed to their code name and I would give it to them in class. Not only did the staff enjoy getting soupy mail, but most of them responded in kind. In class, we went over what they had written.

Thus, after reading a song, a series of letters (several from the staff), and writing two themselves, the students had had a lot of reading and composition practice, as well as vocabulary expansion.

And it all started with a song and video clip! I also composed a Jazz chant with the same words, which, however, they didn't much appreciate. It was perhaps too irreverent, or the material was beginning to get old (I was over-exploiting a good thing). Of course all of these activities were spread over several days.

SWAK letters

July 1

Dear Marsha

It was nice getting to know you this year in school. I will miss you this summer and think of you often. Our conversations were the best part of school for me. I hope we can continue to see each other in September. Have a nice summer.

your friend,
John

July 8

Dearest Marsha,

I have only been away from you for one week. I miss you already. I think of you all the time. I wish you were here. I hope the summer goes quickly so I can see you again. Do you think of me sometimes?

fondly, hugs, John

July 15

Marsha, my love,

I've begun dreaming of you every night. I see you in the sunset. Your eyes are like the sky. Your hair is like cornflakes. Your smile is like the sunlight. Your voice is sweet like the song of birds. I long to touch your skin like honey. Your breath is the warm summer breeze. I love you so much. I am desperate. Please write or I shall die. I miss you more than you will ever know.

Kisses and hugs with all my love, John

July 21

My only true love, my precious Marsha,

I've decided. I want you, and only you, for always. Will you be my girl? We could have a lovely family. I would do anything for you. I adore you. Your lovely eyes are like the ocean. Your mouth like a cherry. Your skin so tender like my soccer ball. I love you, I need you. I want to hold you tenderly. I can't live without you. I want to be with you now. We'll be together forever.

Your adoring John

July 25

Dear John,

I just received your letter of July 1 because I am on vacation at Loveboat Beach. It was so sweet of you to think of me. But I must admit that this is the first time that I have thought of you or school. I've been having so much fun. I've been going out with a different boy almost every night. And they are all so strong and handsome. Now I am in love with one particular boy, he's the lifeguard at the beach. I'll tell you all about him when we meet again in September. Take care of yourself and have a nice summer.

Your friend,
Marsha

Questions on the SWAK letters:

1 How many letters are there?
   About how many days apart were they written?
2 How many are from John and how many from Marsha?
3 How many letters did Marsha receive before she wrote her letter?
4 How does John describe Marsha's voice/hair/mouth/breath/eyes/ smile/skin: *It's like the . . .*
5 John has become infatuated with Marsha. How does Marsha feel about him?
6 What kind of boys does Marsha like?
7 Who is she in love with now?
8 What do you think will happen in September?
9 If you were to advise John and Marsha, what would you tell them (did they do anything wrong in their correspondence)?

After I had written this case history, I used the same video clip again in Japan during the summer of 1991, and asked my students to write secret postcards to each other.

5   Testing with songs

Songs, like any texts, can be used to evaluate and test. In fact, students usually feel more secure about learning with songs when the material in them is actually tested conventionally. This gives them the academic 'stamp of approval' and allows them to be treated more seriously, as they should be.

I have used several methods to test students. The most interesting to me consists of asking the students to list what new vocabulary they have learned from a corpus of songs. They give you their lists and you go over them together deciding the following points:

1 What words or expression are not worth learning. (*Gee Whiz* in *Dream, Dream, Dream*)
2 Which ones they already know and
3 Which ones they need help with from the teacher.

I compile their lists on a hand-out and give them class time to talk to each other about what the words mean; and to ask me if nobody else knows. The students feel good about it because they have picked the things that they feel are important for them to learn and because basically they have created the test. Later, when they are given the test, they know what is going to be on it. Furthermore, it often is testing material that they have contributed to the course, and so they feel pleased with their self-directed learning.

Students can also write content questions for themselves on the songs and when given different test types (as below) they write other types of questions.

Options for testing vocabulary and composition

1 Ask the students to translate.

2 Ask them to define.

3 Give a list of expressions, idiomatic and other, from songs that have been worked with in class, and ask the students to put them into a context (a story) in which their meaning becomes clear.

4 Gap-fill: In *VOcable*, Rogers and Olorenshaw suggest a Pop Lyrics Quiz in which lines of songs are given with blanks (for example, I can't get no . . . . (Rolling Stones)) The artists are given as a clue. A list of possibilities can be given at the bottom of a hand-out for lower-level classes.

Options for testing content and composition skills

1 Comprehension: Questions stemming from either an article or one of many kinds of hit parade listing, or from songs themselves.

2 Multiple choice: Who won the 1983 Best Video Award?
a) Madonna

b) Michael Jackson
c) Sting
d) Bruce Springsteen

3 Analysis: Pick one of the three song texts below and comment on its poetic features and structure.

4 Essay: (For example) Summarize Sting's *Russians* and react personally to it. Some of the questions you might want to consider are:
Do you think the song is effective?
Do you think there are many people who understand it?
How will it change things if at all?
Was Sting just trying to get media attention? etc.

Options for testing listening comprehension

1 Gap-fill: This is, of course, the easiest option and the most common. But there could be questions concerning global understanding, instrumentation, etc. Questions can be given out before playing the song to encourage selective listening or afterwards to test more holistic listening.

2 Dictation: Either you read the lyrics, or play a song and use the pause button a lot.

3 Oral exam: Students are asked specific or open-ended questions about the songs used in class, the vocabulary and expressions, or their music and song use in general.

Often students can relax a bit more during such testing since the subject matter is familiar to them. Songs are already being used for testing in some commercial schools in Switzerland and at my university in Japan. There, we record part of a song and then two native speakers have a short impromptu conversation concerning the song and their feelings and impressions about it. Holistic comprehension questions are then made based upon the recording.

I am convinced that testing can be a positive learning experience and does not need to be, as it so often is, simply a negative evaluation. Recently, I had students mark (on a student-compiled list) the terms and expressions they were not sure of, and I told them to study only those for the test. When they came in for the test, pairs simply exchanged papers and asked each other to explain the terms that were marked. They were given a grade based upon the number they knew. That way only what was unknown was studied then tested, and hopefully further learned in the process of testing. What was already known was not tested. That, to me, is much more efficient.

Annotated bibliography

For teaching English

Abbs, B. and **T. Jones.** 1977. *Cloudsongs*. Harlow: Longman. (Cassette, record, songsheets. Beginner, secondary–adult.)

Abbs, B. and **N. York.** 1975. *Skyhigh*, Harlow: Longman. (Cassette, record, songsheets. Intermediate, secondary–adult.)

Abe, K. and **M. Marquardt.** 1988. (eds.). *Let's Sing Together*. Tokyo: Kyobundo. (Two cassettes, book. Beginner–children.)

Attwood, T. and **P. Farmer.** 1978. *Pop Workbook*. London: Edward Arnold (For native British youth in Social Studies or Music lessons, historical and critical analysis of pop music.)

Beall, P. and **S. Nipp.** 1979. *Wee Sing*. Los Angeles: Price Stern Sloan. This a series for native-speaking children of traditional songs, finger plays, and song games. Nicely recorded with children's voices and instrumentation. There are eight different sets in the materials, each with a cassette and booklet of songs with musical notation. Also available are eleven *Wee Sing* books which combine colouring, and five videos in the series. for catalogue write to Price Stern Sloan P.O. Box 21942, Los Angeles, CA 90021, USA.

Biederstädt, W. 1987. *Songs of Our Time*. Stuttgart: Klett. (Student's book with readings, exercises, and glossary; teacher's book; cassette. The best contemporary collection of songs adapted for EFL, in my opinion. Highly usable in class. I look forward to further such collections in the near future!)

Bludau, M. 1973/1981. *Pop-texts and analysis*. Dortmund: Lensing. (A booklet of songs and articles about pop, artists, and their social impact; contains several contradictory accounts of the same event from various journalists, which encourages a critical evaluation of the mass media. For rather mature and advanced students.)

Bostock, P. 1972. *Dialogues and Songs*. Walton-on-Thames: Nelson. (Two cassettes. Beginner, secondary.)

British Broadcasting Corporation using songs: *Pop Words, Catch the Words, Pedagogical Pop, Pop Talk, Remember the Words, Folkangle, Singalong*. (Contact: BBC, PO Box 76, Bush House, The Strand, London WCB 4PH.)

Bushnell, G., F. Morel, and **R. Thomas.** 1981. *Songswork One* and *Songswork Two*. Paris: Berlin. (Cassette, teacher's and student's book. Beginner, elementary–secondary.)

Byrne, J. and **A. Waugh.** 1982. *Jingle Bells and Other Songs*. Oxford: Oxford University Press. (Traditional songs for young learners. Book, cassette.)

Carrier, M. and **C. Evans.** 1981. *The Pop Industry.* Graded reader level 5. London: Cassell.

Case, D. *et al.* 1976. *Singlish: A graded series of English Teaching Songs.* London: British Broadcasting Corporation, English by Radio and Television. (Book, two cassettes. Beginner.)

Dakin, J. 1967. *Songs and Rhymes for the Teaching of English.* London: Longman. (Pupils' and teacher's books, record. Beginner–pre-intermediate, primary.)

Dougill, J. 1989. *Rock Classics.* London: Macmillan. (A simple reader covering eighteen 'greats' of rock, from Elvis Presley to Madonna. Good picture and song lyrics, with notes in Japanese in the Japanese edition.)

Edmundson, D. and **M. Frankel.** 1974. *Sing Along.* Harlow: Longman. (Cassette, record, traditional songs to accompany the *Look, Listen and Learn* course, but can be used independently. Beginner, primary.)

Gibitz, U. 1979. *Sing along with us.* Frankfurt: Hirschgraben Verlag. (Cassette, workbook, accompanies the course *Anyway.* Made for EFL songs.)

Graham, C. 1978. *Jazz Chants.* New York: Oxford University Press. (Workbook, cassette. Beginner–intermediate.)

Graham, C. 1979. *Jazz Chants for Children.* New York: Oxford University Press. (Workbook, cassette, and teacher's book. Beginner.)

Graham, C. 1987. *Small Talk.* New York: Oxford University Press. (Workbook, cassette.)

Graham, C. 1988. *Fairytale Jazz Chants.* New York: Oxford University Press. (Workbook, cassette. Children.)

Gray, P. 1991. 'Using songs in the English conversation classroom'. *Academia,* Seishu Junior College (Sapporo) 22: 69–75.

Grenough, M. 1976. *Sing It!* New York: McGraw-Hill. (Cassette, teacher's and student's book. Beginner–advanced; elementary–adult.)

Hass and **Hong.** 1986. *Rock- und Popsongs im Englischunterricht.* Munich: Manz Verlag.

Harmer, J. 1974. *English Tea.* London: Macmillan. (Record, songsheets, accompanies the *Context English* series but can be used independently. Beginner–intermediate; secondary–adult.)

Jones, C. 1980. *Back Home.* Harlow: Longman. (Record, cassette, accompanies the *Mainline Beginners B* course but can be used independently. Beginner–secondary; adult.)

Kahl, P. and **H. Schutt.** (eds.). 1965. *It's Fun to Sing.* Frankfurt: Diesterweg.

Kind, U. 1980. *Tune In To English.* New York: Regents. (Useful words rewritten to well-known melodies.)

Kinsbury, R. and **P. O'Shea.** 1973. *Sunday Afternoons.* London: Longman Group Ltd. (Cassette, teacher's notes. Elementary–intermediate.)

Kinsbury, R. and **O'Shea, P.** 1979. *Seasons and People, and other Songs.* Oxford: Oxford University Press. (Cassette, songbook pack. Elementary; secondary.)

Knight, M. and **R. Ridout.** (eds.). 1979. *Evans Graded Verse: Songs, Rhymes, and Poems for Students of English.* London: Evans. (Five books, teacher's guides, three cassettes.)

Kroher, O. 1974. *Sing Out!* Stuttgart: Klett. (Traditional Anglo-American songs with translations and notes. Cassette, tape, or LP.)

Lander, S. 1988. Things to do with songs in the EFL classroom. *English Teachers Association* (Switzerland) *Newsletter.* 5/3: 3–17.

Lee, W. and **M. Dodderidge.** 1963. *Time for a Song: A Book of Songs for Overseas Learners of English.* Harlow: Longman. (Beginner; primary.)

Linde, C. (ed.). 1988. *Folksongs aus America.* Frankfurt am M.: Fischer.

Marcheteau, M., J. Parker-Brown, M. Sampson, and **D. Barda** 1989. *L'Anglais par les Chansons: Chants traditionnels de Grande-Bretagne, d'Irlande et des Etats-Unis.* Paris: Presses Pocket.

Merdinger, P. and **J. Rosenfeld.** 1984. *Even If You Can't Carry A Tune: Grammar through Popular Songs.* Rowley, Mass.: Newbury House. (Book, cassette, original recordings, well organized.)

My English Songbook. 1981. University of York and Macmillan. (Book, tape, cassette. Beginner–elementary; primary–secondary.)

Murphey, T. 1981. *Foreign Situation.* Gainesville, Fla.: Windy Rock Music. (Cassette, workbook, original songs.)

Osman, A. and **J. McConochie.** 1979. *If You Feel Like Singing.* New York: Longman. (28 American folksongs, book with interesting cultural readings and exercises, cassette. Intermediate; secondary–adult.)

The Otter's First Song Collection: Songs for Children. 1985. Ditchling, Sussex: Otter Sound Limited (Book and cassette.)

Papa, M. and **G. Iantorno.** 1986. *Famous British and American Songs: and their cultural background.* London: Longman. (Book, cassette. Elementary–advanced; secondary–adult.)

Rabley, S. 1989. *The Youth Culture.* London: Macmillan. (has a good section on rock and pop, and other related materials. Excellent layout.)

Russel-Smith, G. 1969. *Kodaly Choral Method: Fifty Nursery Songs.* London: Boosey and Hawkes.

Schneider, B. 1987. *Sharing a Song*. Reading, Mass.: Addison-Wesley. (Three cassettes, teacher's and student's book. Beginner–intermediate; elementary.)

Spaventa, L. (no date). *Ten Tales in Song*. Canterbury: Pilgrims Language Courses. (Student's book, teacher's book, cassette. Elementary–advanced; secondary–adult.

Tomalin, B. 1977. *Songs Alive: English through Traditional Songs*. London: BBC, English by Radio and Television. (Ten 15-minute TV programmes available on video or film, cassette recording, book. Intermediate; secondary.)

Ward, S. 1980. *Dippitydoo: Songs and Activities for Children*. Harlow: Longman. (Cassette, workbook, and teacher's guide. Beginners; elementary 6–10.)

Wellman, L. and **D. Byrd**. 1975. *Hard to Learn that English as a Second Language Blues*. New York: Collier Macmillan International, Inc. (Cassette recording. Intermediate; secondary.)

Wellman, L. and **D. Byrd**. (1976). *ESL Express*. New York: Collier Macmillan International, Inc. (Cassette recording. Beginner; secondary.)

Wilson, K. 1972. *Mister Monday and Other Songs for the Teaching of English.* Harlow: Longman. (Cassette recording, teacher's notes. Secondary–adult.)

Wilson, K. 1974. *Goodbye Rainbow*. Harlow: Longman. (Cassette recording, teacher's notes. Intermediate; secondary–adult.)

Wilson, K. 1979. *Same Time, Same Place*. Harlow: Longman. (Cassette recording, songsheets. Accompanies the *Mainline Beginners A* course but can be used independently. Beginner; secondary–adult.)

Wilson, K. 1979. *My Friend Jack: new songs for English*. Berlin: Cornelsen-Velhagen and Klasing. (Cassette recording or tape and booklet.)

Zacher, P. and **K. Eulitz**. (eds.) 1987 *Sing a Song: Songs of Peoples in North America.* Stuttgart: Klett Verlag. (Collection of traditional songs, translations in German. Cassette 'Sing Out'.)

In the Japanese market

Fukuda, S. and **A. Rosen**. 1982. *Understanding Rock*. Toyko: Taishukan.

Fukuda, S. and **A. Rosen**. 1983. *Understanding Rock 2*. Tokyo: Taishukan.

Fukuda S. and **A. Rosen**. 1985. *Understanding Rock 3*. Tokyo: Taishukan. (Each of the above three books contains lyrics of twenty American and British popular songs from the 1960s to 1985. These are transcribed as sung, and translated and explained in Japanese, with poetic sociocultural information, and pattern practice in useful linguistic elements.)

Fukuda, S. and **A. Rosen.** 1986. *English through the Beatles*. Tokyo: Taishukan.

Hayashi, I. 1977. *Beatles de Egio wo Manabo*. Tokyo: Taishukan.

Biederstädt, W. 1990. *Cries of young souls: songs that speak to you*. (ed.) Japanese editor/annotator Masaaki Ohsugi. Tokyo: Asahi Press. (This is a Japanese version of Biederstädt's popular *Songs of Our time*. Klett.)

Video

Battle and Hum – by U2, Paramount Pictures Corporation, Island Records, 1988. There is also a book available. Excellent footage of Bono talking and singing through *Sunday, Bloody Sunday*. 99 minutes.

Muzzy in Gondoland – BBC Video course for young children with one 75-minute video, audio cassette, six activity booklets, a workbook, song book, teachers'/parents' notes.

Playtime – by H. Gottschalk. München: TR Verlagsunion. Two video cassettes and two audio cassettes – programmes aired on Swiss television.

Rolling Stone: 20 Years of Rock n' Roll – Straight Arrow Publishers, EMI. Contains lots of hit songs and good interview material. 98 minutes.

Sesame Street – CBS / Sony. Provides a range of materials using music and jazz-chant type of music. Successful with children and adults.

Songs Alive – BBC, ten quarter-hour units using traditional songs from England, Scotland, Ireland, Australia, and America. Book for students and teacher. Audio cassette.

The Magic Music Man – OUP 1988. The copy of the audio cassette of songs is pedagogically impressive and pleasant.

Cooper, R., M. Lavery, and **M. Rinvolucri.** 1991. *Video* Oxford: Oxford University Press. A resource book with many useful hints on pro-active video use in the classroom.

Sources cited and background reading

Asher, J. 1965. 'The strategy of total physical response: an application to learning Russian'. *International Review of Applied Linguistics* 3:292–9

Asher, J. 1977 *Learning Another Language Through Actions: The Complete Teacher's Guide*. Los Gatos, California: Sky Oaks Publications.

Bancroft, W. 1982. 'The Tomatis Method and Suggestopaedia: A Comparative Study'. Paper presented at the International Conference of the Society for Accelerative Learning and Teaching (7th, Colorado, April 30–May 2.)

Blacking, J. 1974. *How Musical is Man?* Seattle and London: University of Washington Press.

Blaukopf, K. and **D. Mark**. (eds.). 1976. *The Cultural Behaviour of Youth*. Unesco.

Booth, M.W. 1981. *The Experience of Songs*. New Haven, Connecticut: Yale University Press.

Brown, S. and **M. Helgesen**. 1989. 'Integrating and extending songs and stories, 1 and 2'. *Practical English Teacher*. Jan/Mar.

Calvet, J-L. 1980. *La chanson dans la classe de français langue étrangère: outils théoriques*. Paris: CLE International.

Davis, P. and **M. Rinvolucri**. 1987. 'Relaxing Dictations'. *SEAL* (summer) *Newsletter*.

Davis, S. 1985. 'Pop lyrics: a mirror and a molder of society'. *Et Cetera* 42:2:167–9.

Davy, D. 1985. *The Use of Songs in EFL Teaching: with special consideration of the pedagogical potential of pop songs*. Dissertation for Diploma of Advanced Studies in Education, University of Lancaster.

Dubin, F. 1974. Pop, rock, and folk music: an overlooked resource. *English Teaching Forum*. July–September: 1–5.

Dubin, F. and **E. Olshtain**. 1977. *Facilitating Language Learning: A Guidebook for the ESL/EFL Teacher*. New York: McGraw Hill.

Frith, S. 1983. *Sound Effects: Youth, Leisure and the Politics of Rock n' Roll*. London: Constable.

Hosokawa, S. 1984. The walkman effect. *Popular Music* 4:165–80.

Julien, J-R. 1987. 'Les scènes du clip: d'un palimpseste saisissable'. *Vibrations* 5:221–8.

Knott, K. 1985. 'From song lyrics to photo-story'. *Practical English Teacher* 5/3: 42–5.

Krashen, S.D. 1985. *The Input Hypothesis*. London: Longman.

Lange, A. 1986. *Stratégies de la musique*. Bruxelles, Pierre Mardaga.

Livingston, F.B. 1973. 'Did the Australopithecines Sing?' *Current Anthropology* 14. No. 1–2: 25–9. (Song before speech theory.)

Lozanov, G. 1978. *Suggestology and Outlines of Suggestopedy*. New York: Gordon and Breach.

Mark, D. (ed.). 1981. *Stock-taking of Musical Life*. Vienna: Doblinger.

Murphey, T. 1989a. *Song and Music in Language Learning: An Analysis of Pop Songs and the Use of Song and Music in Teaching*

English as a Foreign Language. Doctoral thesis, Université de Neuchâtel, Switzerland, 1989. Published by Peter Lange Verlag, Bern, Switzerland, 1990. (European University Studies Series XI, vol 422.)

Murphey, T. 1989b. 'The when, where and who of pop lyrics: the listeners' prerogative'. *Popular Music* 8/2: 185–93.

Murphey, T. 1990. 'The song stuck in my head phenomenon: a melodic din in the LAD?' *System* 18:1, 53–64.

Murphey, T. and **J.L. Alber**. 1985. 'A pop song register: the motherese of adolescence as affective foreigner talk'. *TESOL Quarterly* 12.

Noll, M. 1988. 'The class has finished but the melody lingers on'. *English Teachers' Association, Switzerland, Newsletter* 5:3:18–9.

Opie, I. and **P. Opie**. 1985. *The Singing Game*. Oxford: Oxford University Press.

Reeve, C. and **J. Williamson**. 1987. 'Look what they've done to my song'. *Modern English Teacher* 14:4:33–6.

Rotzoll, K.B. 1985. 'Advertisements' in T.A. van Dijk (ed.): *Discourse and Communication, new approaches to the analyses of mass media discourse and communication*. Berlin: de Gruyter, pp. 94–105.

Rousseau, J.J. 1781/1968. *Essai sur L'Origine des Langues: où il est parlé de la mélodie et de l'imitation musicale*. Bordeaux: Guy Ducros.

Ryding, A. 1985. Songs in short bursts. *Practical English Teaching*, June, p.53.

Sachs, O. 1986. *The Man Who Mistook His Wife for a Hat*. London: Pan Books.

Schiffler, L. 1986. 'Recherche empirique sur l'effet de la musique dans l'enseignement suggestopédique du français'. *Rassegna Italiana di Linguistica Applicata*. 18/2: 65–82.

Sloboda, J. 1985. *The Musical Mind: the cognitive pyschology of music*. Oxford: Clarendon Press.

Stevick, E.W. 1971. *Adapting and Writing Language Lessons*. Washington D.C.: Government Printing Office.

Strudel, L. 1987. 'Three different versions of the concert season in France, East Germany, and the United States'. *TESOL France News* 7/2: 21–4.

Tagg, P. 1979. *Kojak – 50 seconds of television music: towards an analysis of affect in music*. Doctoral disssertation, University of Gotenborg, Sweden.

Thomas, J. 1984. 'Cross-cultural discourse as 'unequal encounter': towards a pragmatic analysis'. *Applied Linguistics*. 5:3:226–35.

Tilaka Sekara, A. 1985. Soundsense. *English Teaching Forum*. Washington D.C.: USIS.

Trudgill, P. 1983. 'Acts of conflicting identity: the sociolinguistics of British pop-song pronunciation' in *On Dialect: Social and Geographical Perspectives.* Oxford: Blackwell. pp. 141–60.

Van Cleve, J. 1984. Using native pop music to enhance the writing process. *TESOL Newsletter* 8:5–6.

Vaney, M. 1988. 'What can you do with music in a foreign language class?' *English Teachers Association* (Switzerland) *Newsletter* 5:3:20–1.